U.S. Department of Transp
Federal Aviation Adminis

MW00479804

Reprint
Jly, 2005

Private Pilot
Rotorcraft, Helicopter and Gyroplane

Practical Test Standards

Flight Standards Service
Washington, DC 20591

NOTE

Material in FAA-S-8081-15A will be effective July 1, 2005. All previous editions of the Private Pilot—Rotorcraft (Helicopter and Gyroplane) Practical Test Standards will be obsolete as of this date.

FOREWORD

The Private Pilot—Rotorcraft (Helicopter and Gyroplane) Practical Test Standards (PTS) book has been published by the Federal Aviation Administration (FAA) to establish the standards for private pilot certification practical tests for the rotorcraft category, helicopter and gyroplane classes. FAA inspectors and designated pilot examiners shall conduct practical tests in compliance with these standards. Flight instructors and applicants should find these standards helpful during training and when preparing for the practical test.

Joseph K. Tintera, Manager
Regulatory Support Division

CONTENTS

SECTION 2: PRIVATE PILOT ROTORCRAFT — GYROPLANE

AREAS OF OPERATION:

INTRODUCTION

General Information

The Flight Standards Service of the Federal Aviation Administration (FAA) has developed this practical test book as the standard that shall be used by FAA inspectors and designated pilot examiners when conducting private pilot rotorcraft practical tests. Flight instructors are expected to use this book when preparing applicants for practical tests. Applicants should be familiar with this book and refer to these standards during their training.

Information considered directive in nature is described in this practical test book in terms, such as "shall" and "must" indicating the actions are mandatory. Guidance information is described in terms, such as "should" and "may" indicating the actions are desirable or permissive but not mandatory.

The FAA gratefully acknowledges the valuable assistance provided by many industry participants who contributed their time and talent in assisting with the revision of these practical test standards.

This practical test standard (PTS) book may be purchased from the Superintendent of Documents, U.S. Government Printing Office (GPO), Washington, DC 20402-9325, or from http://bookstore.gpo.gov. This PTS is also available for download, in pdf format, from the Flight Standards Service web site at http://av-info.faa.gov.

This PTS is published by the U.S. Department of Transportation, Federal Aviation Administration, Airman Testing Standards Branch, AFS-630, P.O. Box 25082, Oklahoma City, OK 73125. Comments regarding this handbook should be sent, in e-mail form, to AFS630comments@faa.gov.

FAA-S-8081-15A

Practical Test Standards Concept

Title 14 of the Code of Federal Regulations (14 CFR) part 61 specifies the areas in which knowledge and skill must be demonstrated by the applicant before the issuance of a Private Pilot Certificate or rating. The CFRs provide the flexibility to permit the FAA to publish practical test standards containing the AREAS OF OPERATION and specific TASKs in which pilot competency shall be demonstrated. The FAA will revise this PTS whenever it is determined that changes are needed in the interest of safety. *Adherence to the provisions of the regulations and the practical test standards is mandatory for the evaluation of private pilot applicants.*

Practical Test Book Description

This test book contains the following Private Pilot Practical Test Standards:

Section 1   Rotorcraft—Helicopter
Section 2   Rotorcraft—Gyroplane

The Private Pilot Rotorcraft Practical Test Standards includes the AREAS OF OPERATION and TASKs for the issuance of an initial Private Pilot Certificate and for the addition of category and/or class ratings to that certificate.

AREAS OF OPERATION are phases of the practical test arranged in a logical sequence within each standard. They begin with Preflight Preparation and end with Postflight Procedures. The examiner may conduct the practical test in any sequence that will result in a complete and efficient test; *however, the ground portion of the practical test shall be accomplished before the flight portion.*

TASKs are titles of knowledge areas, flight procedures, or maneuvers appropriate to an AREA OF OPERATION.

NOTE is used to emphasize special considerations required in the AREA OF OPERATION or TASK.

REFERENCE identifies the publication(s) that describe(s) the TASK. Descriptions of TASKS are not included in the standards because this information can be found in the current issue of the listed reference. Publications other than those listed may be used for references if their content conveys substantially the same meaning as the referenced publications.

These practical test standards are based on the following references.

14 CFR part 43	Maintenance, Preventive Maintenance, Rebuilding, and Alteration
14 CFR part 61	Certification: Pilots and Flight Instructors
14 CFR part 67	Medical Standards and Certification
14 CFR part 91	General Operating and Flight Rules
NTSB Part 830	Notification and Reporting of Aircraft Accidents and Incidents
AC 00-6	Aviation Weather
AC 00-45	Aviation Weather Services
FAA-H-8083-1	Aircraft Weight and Balance Handbook
FAA-H-8083-21	Rotorcraft Flying Handbook
FAA-H-8083-25	Pilot's Handbook of Aeronautical Knowledge
AC 60-22	Aeronautical Decision Making
AC 60-28	English Language Skill Standards Required by 14 CFR parts 61,63, and 65
AC 61-65	Certification: Pilots and Flight Instructors and Ground Instructors
AC 61-84	Role of Preflight Preparation
AC 61-134	General Aviation Controlled Flight into Terrain Awareness
AC 90-48	Pilots' Role in Collision Avoidance
AC 90-87	Helicopter Dynamic Rollover
AC 90-95	Unanticipated Right Yaw in Helicopters
AC 91-13	Cold Weather Operation of Aircraft
AC 91-32	Safety In and Around Helicopters
AC 91-42	Hazards of Rotating Propeller and Helicopter Rotor Blades
AC 91-55	Reduction of Electrical System Failures following Aircraft Engine Starting
AIM	Aeronautical Information Manual
AFD	Airport Facility Directory
FDC NOTAMs	National Flight Data Center Notices to Airmen
OTHER	Pertinent Pilot's Operating Handbooks FAA-Approved Flight Manuals Navigation Charts

The Objective lists the important elements that must be satisfactorily performed to demonstrate competency in a TASK. The Objective includes:

1. specifically what the applicant should be able to do;
2. the conditions under which the TASK is to be performed; and
3. the acceptable standards of performance.

Abbreviations

14 CFR	Title 14 of the Code of Federal Regulations
ADM	Aeronautical Decision Making
AIRMETS	Airman's Meteorological Information
ATC	Air Traffic Control
ATIS	Automatic Terminal Information Service
ATS	Air Traffic Service
CFIT	Controlled Flight Into Terrain
CRM	Cockpit Resource Management
FAA	Federal Aviation Administration
FSDO	Flight Standards District Office
GPO	Government Printing Office
NAVAID	Navigation Aid
NDB	Non-directional Beacon (Automatic Direction Finder)
NOTAM	Notice to Airmen
NWS	National Weather Service
PTS	Practical Test Standard
SIGMETS	Significant Meteorological Advisory

Use of the Practical Test Standards

The Private Pilot Rotorcraft Practical Test Standards are designed to evaluate competency in both knowledge and skill.

The FAA requires that all practical tests be conducted in accordance with the appropriate practical test standards and the policies set forth in this INTRODUCTION. Private pilot applicants shall be evaluated in **ALL** TASKS included in each AREA OF OPERATION of the appropriate practical test standard, unless otherwise noted.

An applicant, who holds at least a Private Pilot Certificate seeking an additional rotorcraft category rating and/or class rating at the private pilot level shall be evaluated in the AREAS OF OPERATION and TASKS listed in the Additional Rating Task Table. At the discretion of the examiner, an evaluation of the applicant's competence in the remaining AREAS OF OPERATION and TASKs may be conducted.

If the applicant holds two or more category or class ratings at least at the private level, and the rating table indicates differing required TASKS, the "least restrictive" entry applies. For example, if "ALL" and "NONE" are indicated for one AREA OF OPERATION, the "NONE" entry applies. If "B" and "B, C" are indicated, the "B" entry applies.

In preparation for each practical test, the examiner shall develop a written "plan of action" for each practical test. The "plan of action" is a tool, for the sole use of the examiner, to be used in evaluating the applicant. The plan of action need not be grammatically correct or in any formal format. The plan of action must contain all of the required AREAS OF OPERATION and TASKs and any optional TASKs selected by the examiner.

The "plan of action" shall incorporate one or more scenarios that will be used during the practical test. The examiner should try to include as many of the TASKs into the scenario portion of the test as possible, but maintain the flexibility to change due to unexpected situations as they arise and still result in an efficient and valid test. *Any TASK selected for evaluation during a practical test shall be evaluated in its entirety.*

The examiner is not required to follow the precise order in which the AREAS OF OPERATION and TASKs appear in this book. The examiner may change the sequence or combine TASKS with similar Objectives to have an orderly and efficient flow of the practical test. For example Radio Communications and ATC Light Signals may be combined with Traffic Patterns. The examiner's "plan of action" shall include the order and combination of TASKs to be demonstrated by the applicant in a manner that will result in an efficient and valid test.

The examiner is expected to use good judgment in the performance of simulated emergency procedures. The use of the safest means for simulation is expected. Consideration must be given to local conditions, both meteorological and topographical, at the time of the test, as well as the applicant's, workload, and the condition of the aircraft used. If the procedure being evaluated would jeopardize safety, it is expected that the applicant shall simulate that portion of the maneuver.

Special Emphasis Areas

Examiners shall place special emphasis upon areas of aircraft operation considered critical to flight safety. Among these are:

1. positive aircraft control;
2. procedures for positive exchange of flight controls (who is flying the aircraft);
3. collision avoidance;
4. wake turbulence avoidance;
5. runway incursion avoidance;
6. CFIT;
7. wire strike avoidance;
8. ADM and risk management;
9. checklist usage; and
10. other areas deemed appropriate to any phase of the practical test.

Although these areas may not be specifically addressed under each TASK, they are essential to flight safety and will be evaluated during the practical test. In all instances, the applicant's actions will relate to the complete situation.

Private Pilot—Rotorcraft Practical Test Prerequisites

An applicant for the Private Pilot Rotorcraft Practical Test is required by 14 CFR part 61 to:

1. be at least 17 years of age;
2. be able to read, speak, write, and understand the English language. If there is a doubt, use AC 60-28, English Language Skill Standards;
3. have passed the appropriate private pilot knowledge test since the beginning of the 24th month before the month in which practical test is completed have satisfactorily accomplished the required training and obtained the aeronautical experience prescribed;
4. possess at least a current Third-Class Medical Certificate;
5. have an endorsement from an authorized instructor certifying that the applicant has received and logged training time within 60 days preceding the date of application; and
6. also have an endorsement certifying that the applicant has demonstrated satisfactory knowledge of the subject areas in which the applicant was deficient on the airman knowledge test.

Aircraft and Equipment Required for the Practical Test

The private pilot rotorcraft applicant is required by 14 CFR part 61, section 61.45 to provide an airworthy, certificated aircraft for use during the practical test. This section further requires that the aircraft must:

1. be of U.S., foreign or military registry of the same category, class, and type, if applicable, for the certificate and/or rating for which the applicant is applying;
2. have fully functioning dual controls, except as provided in 14 CFR part 61, section 61.45(c) and (e); and
3. be capable of performing ALL AREAS OF OPERATION appropriate to the rating sought and have no operating limitations, which prohibit its use in any of the AREAS OF OPERATION, required for the practical test.

Flight Instructor Responsibility

An appropriately rated flight instructor is responsible for training the private pilot applicant to acceptable standards in **ALL** subject matter areas, procedures, and maneuvers included in the TASKS within the appropriate Private Pilot Practical Test Standard.

Because of the impact of their teaching activities in developing safe, proficient pilots, flight instructors should exhibit a high level of knowledge, skill, and the ability to impart that knowledge and skill to students. Additionally, the flight instructor must certify that the applicant is able to perform safely as a private pilot and is competent to pass the required practical test.

Throughout the applicant's training, the flight instructor is responsible for emphasizing the performance of effective visual scanning, collision avoidance, and runway incursion avoidance procedures. These areas are covered, in part, in AC 90-48, Pilot's Role in Collision Avoidance; FAA-H-8083-25, Pilot's Handbook of Aeronautical Knowledge; and the Aeronautical Information Manual.

Examiner[1] Responsibility

The examiner conducting the practical test is responsible for determining that the applicant meets the acceptable standards of knowledge and skill of each TASK within the appropriate practical test standard. Since there is no formal division between the "oral" and "skill" portions of the practical test, this becomes an ongoing process throughout the test. Oral questioning, to determine the applicant's knowledge of TASKs and related safety factors, should be used judiciously at all times, especially during the flight portion of the practical test.

Examiners shall test to the greatest extent practicable the applicant's correlative abilities rather than mere rote enumeration of facts throughout the practical test.

If the examiner determines that a TASK is incomplete, or the outcome uncertain, the examiner may require the applicant to repeat that TASK, or portions of that TASK. This provision has been made in the interest of fairness and does not mean that instruction, practice, or the repeating of an unsatisfactory TASK is permitted during the certification process.

Throughout the flight portion of the practical test, the examiner shall evaluate the applicant's use of visual scanning and collision avoidance procedures.

---

[1] The word "examiner" denotes either the FAA inspector or FAA designated pilot examiner who conducts the practical test.

FAA-S-8081-15A

Satisfactory Performance

Satisfactory performance to meet the requirements for certification is based on the applicant's ability to safely:

1. perform the TASKs specified in the AREAS OF OPERATION for the certificate or rating sought within the approved standards;
2. demonstrate mastery of the aircraft with the successful outcome of each TASK performed never seriously in doubt;
3. demonstrate satisfactory proficiency and competency within the approved standards;
4. demonstrate sound judgment and ADM; and
5. demonstrate single-pilot competence if the aircraft is type certificated for single-pilot operations.

Unsatisfactory Performance

The tolerances represent the performance expected in good flying conditions. If, in the judgment of the examiner, the applicant does not meet the standards of performance of any TASK performed, the associated AREA OF OPERATION is failed and therefore, the practical test is failed.

The examiner or applicant may discontinue the test at any time when the failure of an AREA OF OPERATION makes the applicant ineligible for the certificate or rating sought. **The test may be continued ONLY with the consent of the applicant.** If the test is discontinued, the applicant is entitled credit for only those AREAS OF OPERATION and their associated TASKs satisfactorily performed. However, during the retest and at the discretion of the examiner, any TASK may be re-evaluated including those previously passed.

Typical areas of unsatisfactory performance and grounds for disqualification are:

1. Any action or lack of action by the applicant that requires corrective intervention by the examiner to maintain safe flight.
2. Failure to use proper and effective visual scanning techniques to clear the area before and while performing maneuvers.
3. Consistently exceeding tolerances stated in the Objectives.
4. Failure to take prompt corrective action when tolerances are exceeded.

When a disapproval notice is issued, the examiner shall record the applicant's unsatisfactory performance in terms of AREA OF OPERATIONS and specific TASK(s) not meeting the standard appropriate to the practical test conducted. The AREA(s) OF OPERATION/TASK(s) not tested and the number of practical test failures shall also be recorded. If the applicant fails the practical test because of a special emphasis area, the Notice of Disapproval shall indicate the associated TASK. i.e.: AREA OF OPERATION VIII, Settling-With-Power, failure to use proper collision avoidance procedures.

Letter of Discontinuance

When a practical test is discontinued for reasons other than unsatisfactory performance (i.e., equipment failure, weather, or illness) FAA Form 8700-1, Airman Certificate and/or Rating Application, and, if applicable, the Airman Knowledge Test Report, shall be returned to the applicant. The examiner at that time shall prepare, sign, and issue a Letter of Discontinuance to the applicant. The Letter of Discontinuance should identify the AREAS OF OPERATION and their associated TASKs of the practical test that were successfully completed. The applicant shall be advised that the Letter of Discontinuance shall be presented to the examiner when the practical test is resumed, and made part of the certification file.

Aeronautical Decision Making and Risk Management

The examiner shall evaluate the applicant's ability throughout the practical test to use good aeronautical decision-making procedures in order to evaluate risks. The examiner shall accomplish this requirement by developing scenarios that incorporate as many TASKs as possible to evaluate the applicants risk management in making safe aeronautical decisions. For example, the examiner may develop a scenario that incorporates weather decisions and performance planning.

The applicant's ability to utilize all the assets available in making a risk analysis to determine the safest course of action is essential for satisfactory performance. The scenarios should be realistic and within the capabilities of the aircraft used for the practical test.

Single-Pilot Resource Management

Single-Pilot Resource Management refers to the effective use of ALL available resources: human resources, hardware, and information. It is similar to Crew Resource Management (CRM) procedures that are being emphasized in multi-crewmember operations except that only one crewmember (the pilot) is involved. Human resources "...includes all other groups routinely working with the pilot who are involved in decisions that are required to operate a flight safely. These groups include, but are not limited to: dispatchers, weather briefers, maintenance personnel, and air traffic controllers." Pilot Resource Management is not a single TASK; it is a set of skill competencies that must be evident in all TASKs in this practical test standard as applied to single-pilot operation.

Applicant's Use of Checklists

Throughout the practical test, the applicant is evaluated on the use of an appropriate checklist. Proper use is dependent on the specific TASK being evaluated. The situation may be such that the use of the checklist, while accomplishing the elements of an Objective, would be either unsafe or impractical, especially in a single-pilot operation. In this case, a review of the checklist after the elements have been accomplished, would be appropriate. Division of attention and proper visual scanning should be considered when using a checklist.

Use of Distractions During Practical Tests

Numerous studies indicate that many accidents have occurred when the pilot has been distracted during critical phases of flight. To evaluate the applicant's ability to utilize proper control technique while dividing attention both inside and/or outside the cockpit, the examiner shall cause a realistic distraction during the flight portion of the practical test to evaluate the applicant's ability to divide attention while maintaining safe flight.

Positive Exchange of Flight Controls

During flight, there must always be a clear understanding between pilots of who has control of the aircraft. Prior to flight, a briefing should be conducted that includes the procedure for the exchange of flight controls. A positive three-step process in the exchange of flight controls between pilots is a proven procedure and one that is strongly recommended.

When one pilot wishes to give the other pilot control of the aircraft, he or she will say, "You have the flight controls." The other pilot acknowledges immediately by saying, "I have the flight controls." The first pilot again says "You have the flight controls." When control is returned to the first pilot, follow the same procedure. A visual check is recommended to verify that the exchange has occurred. There should never be any doubt as to who is flying the aircraft.

FAA-S-8081-15A

SECTION 1

PRIVATE PILOT
ROTORCRAFT – HELICOPTER

Practical Test Standards

CONTENTS: SECTION 1

Addition of a Rotorcraft/Helicopter rating to an existing Private Pilot Certificate

Area of Operation	Required TASKS are indicated by either the TASK letter(s) that apply(s) or an indication that all or none of the TASKS must be tested.								
	PRIVATE PILOT RATING(S) HELD								
	ASEL	ASES	AMEL	AMES	RG	Non-Power Glider	Power Glider	Free Balloon	Airship
I	E,F,G	E,F,G	E,F,G	E,F,G	E,F,G	E,F,G,	E,F,G,	E,F,G,	E,F,G
II	ALL	ALL	ALL	ALL	ALL	ALL	ALL	ALL	ALL
III	B,C	B,C	B,C	B,C	ALL	ALL	ALL	ALL	B,C
IV	ALL	ALL	ALL	ALL	ALL	ALL	ALL	ALL	ALL
V	ALL	ALL	ALL	ALL	ALL	ALL	ALL	ALL	ALL
VI	ALL	ALL	ALL	ALL	ALL	ALL	ALL	ALL	ALL
VII	NONE	NONE	NONE	NONE	B	B,C,D	B,C,D	B,C,D	NONE
VIII	ALL	ALL	ALL	ALL	ALL	ALL	ALL	ALL	ALL
IX	NONE	NONE	NONE	NONE	NONE	ALL	ALL	ALL	ALL
X	ALL	ALL	ALL	ALL	ALL	ALL	ALL	ALL	ALL

TASK VS. SIMULATION DEVICE CREDIT

Examiners conducting the Private Pilot Helicopter Practical Tests with simulation devices should consult appropriate documentation to ensure that the device has been approved for training. The documentation for each device should reflect that the following activities have occurred:

1. The device must be evaluated, determined to meet the appropriate standards, and assigned the appropriate qualification level by the National Simulator Program Manager. The device must continue to meet qualification standards through continuing evaluations as outlined in the appropriate AC. For helicopter simulators, AC 120-63 (as amended), Helicopter Simulator Qualification, will be used.

2. The FAA must approve the device for specific TASKs.

3. The device must continue to support the level of student or applicant performance required by this PTS.

NOTE: Users of the following chart are cautioned that use of the chart alone is incomplete. The description and objective of each TASK as listed in the body of the PTS, including all notes, must also be incorporated for accurate simulation device use.

USE OF CHART

X   Creditable.

X1   Creditable only if accomplished in conjunction with a running takeoff or running landing, as appropriate.

NOTE: 1. The helicopter may be used for all TASKs.
        2. Level C simulators may be used as indicated only if the applicant meets established pre-requisite experience requirements.
        3. Level A helicopter simulator standards have not been defined.
        4. Helicopter flight training devices have not been defined.

FLIGHT TASK
Areas of Operation:

FLIGHT SIMULATION DEVICE LEVEL

	1	2	3	4	5	6	7	A	B	C	D
II. **Preflight Procedures**											
A. Preflight Inspection (Cockpit Only)		—	—	—	—	—	—	—	—	—	—
B. Cockpit Management		—	—	—	—	—	—	—	—	—	—
C. Engine Starting and Rotor Engagement		—	—	—	—	—	—	—	—	—	—
D. Before Takeoff Check		—	—	—	—	—	—	—	—	—	—
III. **Airport and Heliport Operations**											
A. Radio Communications and ATC Light Signals		—	—	—	—	—	—	—	—	—	—
B. Traffic Patterns		—	—	—	—	—	—	—	—	—	—
C. Airport/Heliport Runway, Heliport, and Taxiway Signs, Markings, and Lighting Markings and Lighting		—	—	—	—	—	—	—	—	—	—
IV. **Hovering Maneuvers**											
A. Vertical Takeoff and Landing		—	—	—	—	—	—	—	—	—	—
B. Slope Operations		—	—	—	—	—	—	—	—	—	—
C. Surface Taxi		—	—	—	—	—	—	—	—	—	—
D. Hover Taxi		—	—	—	—	—	—	—	—	—	—
E. Air Taxi		—	—	—	—	—	—	—	—	—	—
V. **Takeoffs, Landings, and Go-Arounds**											
A. Normal and Crosswind Takeoff and Climb		—	—	—	—	—	—	—	—	—	—
B. Normal and Crosswind Approach		—	—	—	—	—	—	—	—	—	—
C. Maximum Performance Takeoff and Climb		—	—	—	—	—	—	—	—	—	—
D. Steep Approach		—	—	—	—	—	—	—	—	—	—
E. Rolling Takeoff		—	—	—	—	—	—	—	—	—	—
F. Confined Area Operations		—	—	—	—	—	—	—	—	—	—
G. Pinnacle/Platform Operations		—	—	—	—	—	—	—	—	—	—
H. Shallow Approach and Running /Roll-On Landing		—	—	—	—	—	—	—	—	—	—
I. Go-Around		—	—	—	—	—	—	—	—	—	—

	1	2	3	4	5	6	7	A	B	C	D
VI. Performance Maneuvers											
A. Rapid Deceleration		—	—	—	—	—	—	—	—	—	—
B. Straight In Autorotations		—	—	—	—	—	—	—	—	—	—
C. 180° Autorotation	—	—	—	—	—	—	—	—	—	—	—
VII. Navigation											
A. Pilotage and Dead Reckoning		—	—	—	—	—	—	—	—	—	—
B. Navigation Systems and Radar Services		—	—	—	—	—	—	—	—	—	—
C. Diversion		—	—	—	—	—	—	—	—	—	—
D. Lost Procedures	—	—	—	—	—	—	—	—	—	—	—
VIII. Emergency Operations											
A. Power Failure at a Hover		—	—	—	—	—	—	—	—	—	X	X
B. Power Failure at Altitude		—	—	—	—	—	—	—	—	—	X	X
C. Systems and Equipment Malfunctions		—	—	—	—	—	—	—	—	—	X	X
D. Settling-With-Power		—	—	—	—	—	—	—	—	—	X	X
E. Low Rotor RPM Recovery		—	—	—	—	—	—	—	—	—	X	X
F. Antitorque System Failure		—	—	—	—	—	—	—	—	—	—	—
G. Dynamic Rollover		—	—	—	—	—	—	—	—	—	—	—
H. Ground Resonance		—	—	—	—	—	—	—	—	—	—	—
I. Low G Conditions		—	—	—	—	—	—	—	—	—	—	—
J. Emergency Equipment and Survival Gear		—	—	—	—	—	—	—	—	—	—	—
X. Postflight Procedures											
A. After Landing and Securing		—	—	—	—	—	—	—	—	—	—	—

FAA-S-8081-15A

APPLICANT'S PRACTICAL TEST CHECKLIST (HELICOPTER)
APPOINTMENT WITH EXAMINER:

EXAMINER'S NAME _____

LOCATION _____

DATE/TIME _____

ACCEPTABLE AIRCRAFT

Aircraft Documents:
    Airworthiness Certificate
    Registration Certificate
    Operating Limitations
Aircraft Maintenance Records:
    Logbook Record of Airworthiness Inspections
    and AD Compliance
Pilot's Operating Handbook and FAA-Approved
    Helicopter Flight Manual
FCC Station License

PERSONAL EQUIPMENT

Current Aeronautical Charts
Computer and Plotter
Flight Plan Form
Flight Logs
Current AIM, Airport Facility Directory, and Appropriate
    Publications

PERSONAL RECORDS

Identification—Photo/Signature ID
Pilot Certificate
Current and Appropriate Medical Certificate
Completed FAA Form 8710-1, Airman Certificate and/or
    Rating Application with Instructor's Signature (if
    applicable)
AC Form 8080-2, Airman Written Test Report or
    Computer Test Report
Pilot Logbook with Appropriate Instructor Endorsements
FAA Form 8060-5, Notice of Disapproval (if applicable)
Approved School Graduation Certificate (if applicable)
Examiner's Fee (if applicable)

        FAA-S-8081-15A

EXAMINER'S PRACTICAL TEST CHECKLIST

(HELICOPTER)

APPLICANT'S NAME _____

LOCATION _____

DATE/TIME _____

I. PREFLIGHT PREPARATION

A. CERTIFICATES AND DOCUMENTS
B. AIRWORTHINESS REQUIRMENTS
C. WEATHER INFORMATION
D. CROSS-COUNTRY FLIGHT PLANNING
E. NATIONAL AIRSPACE SYSTEM
F. PERFORMANCE AND LIMITATIONS
G. OPERATION OF SYSTEMS
H. AEROMEDICAL FACTORS

II. PREFLIGHT PROCEDURES

A. PREFLIGHT INSPECTION
B. COCKPIT MANAGEMENT
C. ENGINE STARTING AND ROTOR ENGAGEMENT
D. BEFORE TAKEOFF CHECK

III. AIRPORT AND HELIPORT OPERATIONS

A. RADIO COMMUNICATIONS AND ATC LIGHT SIGNALS
B. TRAFFIC PATTERNS
C. AIRPORT/HELIPORT RUNWAY, HELIPAD, AND TAXIWAY SIGNS, MARKINGS, AND LIGHTING

IV. HOVERING MANEUVERS

A. VERTICAL TAKEOFF AND LANDING
B. SLOPE OPERATIONS
C. SURFACE TAXI
D. HOVER TAXI
E. AIR TAXI

FAA-S-8081-15A

V. TAKEOFFS, LANDINGS, AND GO-AROUNDS

- **A.** NORMAL AND CROSSWIND TAKEOFF AND CLIMB
- **B.** NORMAL AND CROSSWIND APPROACH
- **C.** MAXIMUM PERFORMANCE TAKEOFF AND CLIMB
- **D.** STEEP APPROACH
- **E.** ROLLING TAKEOFF
- **F.** CONFINED AREA OPERATIONS
- **G.** PINNACLE/PLATFORM OPERATIONS
- **H.** SHALLOW APPROACH AND RUNNING ROLL-ON LANDING
- **I.** GO-AROUND

VI. PERFORMANCE MANEUVERS

- **A.** RAPID DECELERATION
- **B.** STRAIGHT IN AUTOROTATION
- **C.** 180° AUTOROTATION

VII. NAVIGATION

- **A.** PILOTAGE AND DEAD RECKONING
- **B.** RADIO NAVIGATION AND RADAR SERVICES
- **C.** DIVERSION
- **D.** LOST PROCEDURES

VIII. EMERGENCY OPERATIONS

- **A.** POWER FAILURE AT A HOVER
- **B.** POWER FAILURE AT ALTITUDE
- **C.** SYSTEMS AND EQUIPMENT MALFUNCTIONS
- **D.** SETTLING-WITH-POWER
- **E.** LOW ROTOR RPM RECOVERY
- **F.** ANTITORQUE SYSTEM FAILURE
- **G.** DYNAMIC ROLLOVER
- **H.** GROUND RESONANCE
- **I.** LOW G CONDITIONS
- **J.** EMERGENCY EQUIPMENT AND SURVIVAL GEAR

IX. NIGHT OPERATION

- **A.** NIGHT PREPARATION

X. POST-FLIGHT PROCEDURES

- **A.** AFTER LANDING AND SECURING

I. AREA OF OPERATION: PREFLIGHT PREPARATION

NOTE: The examiner shall develop a scenario based on real time weather to evaluate TASKs C, D, E, and F.

A. TASK: CERTIFICATES AND DOCUMENTS

REFERENCES: 14 CFR parts 43, 61, 67, 91; FAA-H-8083-21, FAA-H-8083-25; POH/RFM.

Objective. To determine that the applicant exhibits knowledge of the elements related to certificates and documents by:

1. Explaining—

   a. private pilot certificate privileges, limitations, and recent flight experience requirements.
   b. medical certificate class and duration.
   c. pilot logbook or flight records.

2. Locating and explaining—

   a. airworthiness and registration certificates.
   b. operating limitations, placards, instrument markings, and POH/RFM.
   c. weight and balance data and equipment list.

B. TASK: AIRWORTHINESS REQUIREMENTS

REFERENCES: 14 CFR part 91; FAA-H-8083-21.

Objective. To determine that the applicant exhibits knowledge of the elements related to airworthiness requirements by:

1. Explaining—

   a. required instruments and equipment for day/night VFR.
   b. procedures and limitations for determining airworthiness of the helicopter with inoperative instruments and equipment with and without an MEL.
   c. requirements and procedures for obtaining a special flight permit.

2. Locating and explaining—

   a. airworthiness directives.
   b. compliance records.
   c. maintenance/inspection requirements.
   d. appropriate record keeping.

C. TASK: WEATHER INFORMATION

REFERENCES: 14 CFR part 91; AC 00-6, AC 00-45, AC 61-84; FAA-H-8083-25; AIM.

Objective. To determine that the applicant:

1. Exhibits knowledge of the elements related to weather information by analyzing weather reports, charts, and forecasts from various sources with emphasis on—

   a. METAR, TAF, and FA.
   b. surface analysis chart.
   c. radar summary chart.
   d. winds and temperature aloft chart.
   e. significant weather prognostic charts.
   f. AWOS, ASOS, and ATIS reports.

2. Makes a competent "go/no-go" decision based on available weather information.

D. TASK: CROSS-COUNTRY FLIGHT PLANNING

REFERENCES: 14 CFR part 91; FAA-H-8083-25; AC 61-84; Navigation Charts; Airport/Facility Directory; FDC NOTAMs; AIM.

Objective. To determine that the applicant:

1. Exhibits knowledge of the elements related to cross-country flight planning by presenting and explaining a pre-planned VFR cross-country flight, as previously assigned by the examiner. On the day of the practical test, the final flight plan shall be to the first fuel stop, based on maximum allowable passengers, baggage, and/or cargo loads using real-time weather.
2. Uses appropriate and current aeronautical charts.
3. Properly identifies airspace, obstructions, and terrain features, including discussion of wire strike avoidance techniques.
4. Selects easily identifiable en route checkpoints.
5. Selects the most favorable altitudes, considering weather conditions and equipment capabilities.
6. Computes headings, flight time, and fuel requirements.
7. Selects appropriate navigation systems/facilities and communication frequencies.
8. Applies pertinent information from FDC NOTAMs, AFD, and other flight publications.
9. Completes a navigation log and simulates filing a VFR flight plan.

E. TASK: NATIONAL AIRSPACE SYSTEM

REFERENCES: 14 CFR parts 71, 91; Navigation Charts; AIM.

Objective.   To determine that the applicant exhibits knowledge of the elements related to the National Airspace System by explaining:

1. Basic VFR Weather Minimums—for all classes of airspace.
2. Airspace classes—their operating rules, pilot certification, and helicopter equipment requirements for the following—

   a. Class A.
   b. Class B.
   c. Class C.
   d. Class D.
   e. Class E.
   f. Class G.

3. Special use airspace and other airspace areas.

F. TASK: PERFORMANCE AND LIMITATIONS

REFERENCES: FAA-H-8083-1, FAA-H-8083-21; AC 61-84, AC 90-95; POH/RFM.

Objective.   To determine that the applicant:

1. Exhibits knowledge of the elements related to performance and limitations by explaining the use of charts, tables, and data to determine performance and the adverse effects of exceeding limitations.
2. Computes weight and balance. Determines the computed weight and center of gravity is within the helicopter's operating limitations and if the weight and center of gravity will remain within limits during all phases of flight.
3. Demonstrates the use of appropriate performance charts, tables, and data.
4. Describes the effects of atmospheric conditions on the helicopter's performance.
5. Understands the cause and effects of retreating blade stall.
6. Considers circumstances when operating within "avoid areas" of the height/velocity diagram.
7. Is aware of situations that lead to loss of tail rotor/antitorque effectiveness (unanticipated yaw).

G. TASK: OPERATION OF SYSTEMS

REFERENCES: FAA-H-8083-21; POH/RFM.

Objective. To determine that the applicant exhibits knowledge of the elements related to the operation of systems on the helicopter provided for the flight test by explaining at least three (3) of the following systems:

1. Primary flight controls, trim, and, if installed, stability control.
2. Powerplant.
3. Main rotor and antitorque.
4. Landing gear, brakes, steering, skids, or floats, as applicable.
5. Fuel, oil, and hydraulic.
6. Electrical.
7. Pitot-static, vacuum/pressure, and associated flight instruments, if applicable.
8. Environmental.
9. Anti-icing, including carburetor heat, if applicable.
10. Avionics equipment.

H. TASK: AEROMEDICAL FACTORS

REFERENCES: FAA-H-8083-25; AIM.

Objective. To determine that the applicant exhibits knowledge of the elements related to aeromedical factors by explaining:

1. The symptoms, causes, effects, and corrective actions of at least three (3) of the following—

   a. hypoxia.
   b. hyperventilation.
   c. middle ear and sinus problems.
   d. spatial disorientation.
   e. motion sickness.
   f. carbon monoxide poisoning.
   g. stress and fatigue.
   h. dehydration.

2. The effects of alcohol, drugs, and over-the-counter drugs.
3. The effects of excesses nitrogen during scuba dives upon a pilot or passenger in flight.

II. AREA OF OPERATION: PREFLIGHT PROCEDURES

A. TASK: PREFLIGHT INSPECTION

REFERENCES: FAA-H-8083-21; POH/RFM.

Objective.   To determine that the applicant:

1. Exhibits knowledge of the elements related to preflight inspection. This shall include which items must be inspected, the reasons for checking each item, and how to detect possible defects.
2. Inspects the helicopter with reference to an appropriate checklist.
3. Verifies the helicopter is in condition for safe flight.

B. TASK: COCKPIT MANAGEMENT

REFERENCES: 14 CFR part 91; POH/RFM.

Objective.   To determine that the applicant:

1. Exhibits knowledge of the elements related cockpit management procedures.
2. Ensures all loose items in the cockpit and cabin are secured.
3. Organizes material and equipment in an efficient manner so they are readily available.
4. Briefs the occupants on the use of safety belts, shoulder harnesses, doors, rotor blade avoidance, and emergency procedures.

C. TASK: ENGINE STARTING AND ROTOR ENGAGEMENT

REFERENCES: FAA-H-8083-21; AC 91-13, AC 91-42, AC 91-55; POH/RFM.

Objective. To determine that the applicant:

1. Exhibits knowledge of the elements related to correct engine starting procedures. This shall include the use of an external power source, starting under various atmospheric conditions.
2. Positions the helicopter properly considering structures, surface conditions, other aircraft, and the safety of nearby persons and property.
3. Utilizes the appropriate checklist for starting procedure.

D. TASK: BEFORE TAKEOFF CHECK

REFERENCES: FAA-H-8083-21; POH/RFM.

Objective. To determine that the applicant:

1. Exhibits knowledge of the elements related to the before takeoff check. This shall include the reasons for checking each item and how to detect malfunctions.
2. Positions the helicopter properly considering other aircraft, wind, and surface conditions.
3. Divides attention inside and outside the cockpit.
4. Ensures that the engine temperature and pressure are suitable for run-up and takeoff.
5. Accomplishes the before takeoff check and ensures that the helicopter is in safe operating condition.
6. Reviews takeoff performance airspeeds, takeoff distances departure, and emergency procedures.
7. Avoids runway incursions and/or ensures no conflict with traffic prior to takeoff.

III. AREA OF OPERATION: AIRPORT AND HELIPORT OPERATIONS

A. TASK: RADIO COMMUNICATIONS AND ATC LIGHT SIGNALS

REFERENCE: 14 CFR part 91; FAA-H-8083-25; AIM.

Objective.   To determine that the applicant:

1. Exhibits knowledge of the elements related to radio communications and ATC light signals.
2. Selects appropriate frequencies.
3. Transmits using recommended phraseology.
4. Acknowledges radio communications and compiles with instructions.

B. TASK: TRAFFIC PATTERNS

REFERENCES: 14 CFR part 91; FAA-H-8083-21; AIM; POH/RFM.

Objective.   To determine that the applicant:

1. Exhibits knowledge of the elements related to traffic patterns. This shall include procedures at airports and heliports with and without operating control towers, prevention of runway incursions, collision avoidance, wake turbulence avoidance, and wind shear.
2. Complies with proper traffic pattern procedures.
3. Maintains proper spacing from other traffic or avoids the flow of fixed wing aircraft.
4. Corrects for wind drift to maintain proper ground track.
5. Maintains orientation with runway/landing area in use.
6. Maintains traffic pattern altitude, ±100 feet and the appropriate airspeed, ±10 knots.

C. TASK: AIRPORT/HELIPORT RUNWAY, HELIPAD, AND TAXIWAY SIGNS, MARKINGS, AND LIGHTING.

REFERENCE: 14 CFR part 91; FAA-H-8083-25; AIM.

Objective.   To determine that the applicant:

1. Exhibits knowledge of the elements related to airport/heliport runway, and taxiway operations with emphasis on runway incursion avoidance.
2. Properly identifies and interprets airport/heliport, runway, and taxiway signs, markings, and lighting.

IV. AREA OF OPERATION: HOVERING MANEUVERS

A. TASK: VERTICAL TAKEOFF AND LANDING

REFERENCES: FAA-H-8083-21; AC 90-95; POH/RFM.

Objective.   To determine that the applicant:

1. Exhibits knowledge of the elements related to a vertical takeoff to a hover and landing from a hover.
2. Ascends to and maintains recommended hovering altitude, and descends from recommended hovering altitude in headwind, crosswind, and tailwind conditions.
3. Maintains RPM within normal limits.
4. Establishes recommended hovering altitude, ±1/2 of that altitude within 10 feet of the surface; if above 10 feet, ±5 feet.
5. Avoids conditions that might lead to loss of tail rotor/antitorque effectiveness.
6. Maintains position within 4 feet of a designated point, with no aft movement.
7. Descends vertically to within 4 feet of the designated touchdown point.
8. Maintains specified heading, ±10°.

B. TASK: SLOPE OPERATIONS

REFERENCES: FAA-H-8083-21; POH/RFM.

Objective.   To determine that the applicant:

1. Exhibits knowledge of the elements related to slope operations.
2. Selects a suitable slope, approach, and direction considering wind effect, obstacles, dynamic rollover avoidance, and discharging passengers.
3. Properly moves toward the slope.
4. Maintains RPM within normal limits.
5. Makes a smooth positive descent to touch the upslope skid on the sloping surface.
6. Maintains positive control while lowering the downslope skid or landing gear to touchdown.
7. Recognizes if slope is too steep and abandons the operation prior to reaching cyclic control stops.
8. Makes a smooth transition from the slope to a stabilized hover parallel to the slope.
9. Properly moves away from the slope.
10. Maintains the specified heading throughout the operation, ±10°.

C. TASK: SURFACE TAXI

NOTE: This TASK applies to only helicopters equipped with wheel-type landing gear.

REFERENCES: FAA-H-8083-21; AIM; POH/RFM.

Objective. To determine that the applicant:

1. Exhibits knowledge of the elements related to surface taxiing.
2. Surface taxies the helicopter from one point to another under headwind, crosswind, and tailwind conditions, with the landing gear in contact with the surface, avoiding conditions that might lead to loss of tail rotor/antitorque effectiveness.
3. Properly uses cyclic, collective, and brakes to control speed while taxiing.
4. Properly positions nosewheel/tailwheel, if applicable, locked or unlocked.
5. Maintains RPM within normal limits.
6. Maintains appropriate speed for existing conditions.
7. Stops helicopter within 4 feet of a specified point.
8. Maintains specified track within ±4 feet.

D. TASK: HOVER TAXI

REFERENCES: FAA-H-8083-21; AIM; POH/RFM.

Objective. To determine that the applicant:

1. Exhibits knowledge of the elements related to hover taxiing.
2. Hover taxies over specified ground references, demonstrating forward, sideward, and rearward hovering and hovering turns.
3. Maintains RPM within normal limits.
4. Maintains specified ground track within ±4 feet of a designated reference on straight legs.
5. Maintains constant rate of turn at pivot points.
6. Maintains position within 4 feet of each pivot point during turns.
7. Makes a 360° pivoting turn, left and right, stopping within 10° of a specified heading.
8. Maintains recommended hovering altitude, ±1/2 of that altitude within 10 feet of the surface, if above 10 feet, ±5 feet.

E. TASK: AIR TAXI

REFERENCES: FAA-H-8083-21; AC 90-95; AIM; POH/RFM.

Objective. To determine that the applicant:

1. Exhibits knowledge of the elements related to air taxiing.
2. Air taxies the helicopter from one point to another under headwind and crosswind conditions.
3. Maintains RPM within normal limits.
4. Selects a safe airspeed and altitude.
5. Maintains desired track and groundspeed in headwind and crosswind conditions, avoiding conditions that might lead to loss of tail rotor/antitorque effectiveness.
6. Maintains a specified altitude, ±10 feet.

V. AREA OF OPERATION: TAKEOFFS, LANDINGS, AND GO-AROUNDS

NOTE: The examiner shall select task A, B, C, D, E, and at least one other TASK.

A. TASK: NORMAL AND CROSSWIND TAKEOFF AND CLIMB

REFERENCES: FAA-H-8083-21; POH/RFM.

NOTE: If a calm wind weather condition exists, the applicant's knowledge of the crosswind elements shall be evaluated through oral testing; otherwise a crosswind takeoff and climb shall be demonstrated.

Objective. To determine that the applicant:

1. Exhibits knowledge of the elements related to normal and crosswind takeoff and climb, including factors affecting performance, to include height/velocity information.
2. Establishes a stationary position on the surface or a stabilized hover, prior to takeoff in headwind and crosswind conditions.
3. Maintains RPM within normal limits.
4. Accelerates to manufacturer's recommended climb airspeed, ±10 knots.
5. Maintains proper ground track with crosswind correction, if necessary.
6. Remains aware of the possibility of wind shear and/or wake turbulence.

B. TASK: NORMAL AND CROSSWIND APPROACH

REFERENCES: FAA-H-8083-21; POH/RFM.

NOTE: If a calm wind weather condition exists, the applicant's knowledge of the crosswind elements shall be evaluated through oral testing; otherwise a crosswind approach and landing shall be demonstrated.

Objective. To determine that the applicant:

1. Exhibits knowledge of the elements related to normal and crosswind approach.
2. Considers performance data, to include height/velocity information.
3. Considers the wind conditions, landing surface, and obstacles.
4. Selects a suitable touchdown point.
5. Establishes and maintains the normal approach angle, and proper rate of closure.
6. Remains aware of the possibility of wind shear and/or wake turbulence.
7. Avoids situations that may result in settling-with-power.
8. Maintains proper ground track with crosswind correction, if necessary.
9. Arrives over the touchdown point, on the surface or at a stabilized hover, ±4 feet.
10. Completes the prescribed checklist, if applicable.

C. TASK: MAXIMUM PERFORMANCE TAKEOFF AND CLIMB

REFERENCES: FAA-H-8083-21; POH/RFM.

Objective.   To determine that the applicant:

1. Exhibits knowledge of the elements related to a maximum performance takeoff and climb.
2. Considers situations where this maneuver is recommended and factors related to takeoff and climb performance, to include height/velocity information.
3. Maintains RPM within normal limits.
4. Utilizes proper control technique to initiate takeoff and forward climb airspeed attitude.
5. Utilizes the maximum available takeoff power.
6. After clearing all obstacles, transitions to normal climb attitude, airspeed, ±10 knots, and power setting.
7. Remains aware of the possibility of wind shear and/or wake turbulence.
8. Maintains proper ground track with crosswind correction, if necessary.

D. TASK: STEEP APPROACH

REFERENCES: FAA-H-8083-21; POH/RFM.

Objective.   To determine that the applicant:

1. Exhibits knowledge of the elements related to a steep approach.
2. Considers situations where this maneuver is recommended and factors related to a steep approach, to include height/velocity information.
3. Considers the wind conditions, landing surface, and obstacles.
4. Selects a suitable termination point.
5. Establishes and maintains a steep approach angle, (15° maximum) and proper rate of closure.
6. Avoids situations that can result in settling-with-power.
7. Remains aware of the possibility of wind shear and/or wake turbulence.
8. Maintains proper ground track with crosswind correction, if necessary.
9. Arrives at the termination point, on the surface or at a stabilized hover, ±4 feet.

E. TASK: ROLLING TAKEOFF

NOTE: This TASK applies only to helicopters equipped with wheel-type landing gear.

REFERENCES: FAA-H-8083-21; POH/RFM.

Objective. To determine that the applicant:

1. Exhibits knowledge of the elements related to a rolling takeoff.
2. Considers situations where this maneuver is recommended and factors related to takeoff and climb performance, to include height/velocity information.
3. Maintains RPM within normal limits.
4. Utilizes proper preparatory technique prior to initiating takeoff.
5. Initiates forward accelerating movement on the surface.
6. Transitions to a normal climb airspeed, ±10 knots, and power setting.
7. Remains aware of the possibility of wind shear and/or wake turbulence.
8. Maintains proper ground track with crosswind correction, if necessary.
9. Completes the prescribed checklist, if applicable.

F. TASK: CONFINED AREA OPERATION

REFERENCES: FAA-H-8083-21; POH/RFM.

Objective. To determine that the applicant:

1. Exhibits knowledge of the elements related to confined area operations.
2. Accomplishes a proper high and low reconnaissance.
3. Selects a suitable approach path, termination point, and departure path.
4. Tracks the selected approach path at an acceptable approach angle and rate of closure to the termination point.
5. Maintains RPM within normal limits.
6. Avoids situations that can result in settling-with-power.
7. Terminates at a hover or on the surface, as conditions allow.
8. Accomplishes a proper ground reconnaissance.
9. Selects a suitable takeoff point, considers factors affecting takeoff and climb performance under various conditions.

G. TASK: PINNACLE/PLATFORM OPERATIONS

REFERENCES: FAA-H-8083-21; POH/RFM.

Objective. To determine that the applicant:

1. Exhibits knowledge of the elements related to pinnacle/platform operations.
2. Accomplishes a proper high and low reconnaissance.
3. Selects a suitable approach path, termination point, and departure path.
4. Tracks the selected approach path at an acceptable approach angle and rate of closure to the termination point.
5. Maintains RPM within normal limits.
6. Terminates at a hover or on the surface, as conditions allow.
7. Accomplishes a proper ground reconnaissance.
8. Selects a suitable takeoff point, considers factors affecting takeoff and climb performance under various conditions.

H. TASK: SHALLOW APPROACH AND RUNNING/ROLL-ON LANDING

REFERENCES: FAA-H-8083-21; POH/RFM.

Objective. To determine that the applicant:

1. Exhibits knowledge of the elements related to shallow approach and running/roll-on landing, including the purpose of the maneuver, factors affecting performance data, to include height/velocity information, and effect of landing surface texture.
2. Maintains RPM within normal limits.
3. Considers obstacles and other hazards.
4. Establishes and maintains the recommended approach angle, and proper rate of closure.
5. Remains aware of the possibility of wind shear and/or wake turbulence.
6. Maintains proper ground track with crosswind correction, if necessary.
7. Maintains a speed that will take advantage of effective translational lift during surface contact with landing gear parallel with the ground track.
8. Utilizes proper flight control technique after surface contact.
9. Completes the prescribed checklist, if applicable.

I. TASK: GO-AROUND

REFERENCES: FAA-H-8083-21; POH/RFM.

Objective. To determine that the applicant:

1. Exhibits knowledge of the elements related to a go-around and when it is necessary.
2. Makes a timely decision to discontinue the approach to landing.
3. Maintains RPM within normal limits.
4. Establishes proper control input to stop descent and initiate climb.
5. Retracts the landing gear, if applicable, after a positive rate-of-climb indication.
6. Maintains proper ground track with crosswind correction, if necessary.
7. Transitions to a normal climb airspeed, ±10 knots.
8. Completes the prescribed checklist, if applicable.

VI. AREA OF OPERATION: PERFORMANCE MANEUVERS

NOTE: The examiner shall select TASK A and at least one other TASK.

A. TASK: RAPID DECELERATION

REFERENCES: FAA-H-8083-21; POH/RFM.

Objective. To determine that the applicant:

1. Exhibits knowledge of the elements related to rapid deceleration.
2. Maintains RPM within normal limits.
3. Properly coordinates all controls throughout the execution of the maneuver.
4. Maintains an altitude that will permit safe clearance between the tail boom and the surface.
5. Decelerates and terminates in a stationary hover at the recommended hovering altitude.
6. Maintains heading throughout the maneuver, ±10°.

B. TASK: STRAIGHT IN AUTOROTATION

REFERENCES: FAA-H-8083-21; POH/RFM.

Objective. To determine that the applicant:

1. Exhibits knowledge of the elements related to a straight in autorotation terminating with a power recovery to a hover.
2. Selects a suitable touchdown area.
3. Initiates the maneuver at the proper point.
4. Establishes proper aircraft trim and autorotation airspeed, ±5 knots.
5. Maintains rotor RPM within normal limits.
6. Compensates for windspeed and direction as necessary to avoid undershooting or overshooting the selected landing area.
7. Utilizes proper deceleration, collective pitch application to a hover.
8. Comes to a hover within 200 feet of a designated point.

C. TASK: 180° AUTOROTATION

REFERENCES: FAA-H-8083-21; POH/RFM.

Objective.   To determine that the applicant:

1. Exhibits knowledge of the elements related to a 180° autorotation terminating with a power recovery to a hover.
2. Selects a suitable touchdown area.
3. Initiates the maneuver at the proper point.
4. Establishes proper aircraft trim and autorotation airspeed, ±5 knots.
5. Maintains rotor RPM within normal limits.
6. Compensates for windspeed and direction as necessary to avoid undershooting or overshooting the selected landing area.
7. Utilizes proper deceleration, collective pitch application to a hover.
8. Comes to a hover within 200 feet of a designated point.

VII. AREA OF OPERATION: NAVIGATION

A. TASK: PILOTAGE AND DEAD RECKONING

REFERENCES: FAA-H-8083-25; AC 61-84.

Objective.   To determine that the applicant:

1. Exhibits knowledge of the elements related to pilotage and dead reckoning.
2. Follows the preplanned course by reference to landmarks.
3. Identifies landmarks by relating the surface features to chart symbols.
4. Navigates by means of precomputed headings, groundspeeds, and elapsed time.
5. Corrects for, and records, the differences between preflight fuel, groundspeed, and heading calculations and those determined en route.
6. Verifies the helicopter's position within three (3) nautical miles of the flight planned route.
7. Arrives at the en route checkpoints within five (5) minutes of the initial or revised ETA and provides a destination estimate.
8. Maintains the appropriate altitude, ±200 feet and established heading, ±15°.

B. TASK: NAVIGATION SYSTEMS AND RADAR SERVICES

REFERENCES: FAA-H-8083-25; AC 61-84; Navigation Equipment Operation Manuals; AIM.

Objective. To determine that the applicant:

1. Exhibits knowledge of the elements related to radio navigation and ATC radar services.
2. Demonstrates the ability to use an airborne electronic navigation system.
3. Locates the helicopter's position using the navigation system.
4. Intercepts and tracks a given course, radial or bearing, as appropriate.
5. Recognizes and describes the indication of station or waypoint passage if appropriate.
6. Recognizes signal loss and takes appropriate action.
7. Uses proper communication procedures when utilizing radar services.
8. Maintains the appropriate altitude, ±200 feet and headings ±15°.

C. TASK: DIVERSION

REFERENCES: FAA-H-8083-21; AIM.

Objective. To determine that the applicant:

1. Exhibits knowledge of the elements related to diversion.
2. Selects an appropriate alternate airport or heliport and route.
3. Promptly, diverts toward the alternate airport or heliport.
4. Makes an accurate estimate of heading, groundspeed, arrival time, and fuel consumption to the alternate airport or heliport.
5. Maintains the appropriate altitude, ±200 feet and established heading, ±15°.

D. TASK: LOST PROCEDURES

REFERENCES: FAA-H-8083-21; AIM.

Objective. To determine that the applicant:

1. Exhibits knowledge of the elements related to lost procedures.
2. Selects an appropriate course of action.
3. Maintains an appropriate heading and climbs, if necessary.
4. Identifies prominent landmark(s).
5. Uses navigation systems/facilities and/or contacts an ATC facility for assistance as appropriate.
6. Plans a precautionary landing if deteriorating weather and/or fuel exhaustion is impending.

VIII. AREA OF OPERATION: EMERGENCY OPERATIONS

NOTE: TASKs F through I are knowledge only TASKs.

A. TASK: POWER FAILURE AT A HOVER

REFERENCES: FAA-H-8083-21; POH/RFM.

Objective. To determine that the applicant:

1. Exhibits knowledge of the elements related to power failure at a hover.
2. Determines that the terrain below the aircraft is suitable for a safe touchdown.
3. Performs autorotation from a stationary or forward hover into the wind at recommended altitude, and RPM, while maintaining established heading, ±10°.
4. Touches down with minimum sideward movement, and no rearward movement.
5. Exhibits orientation, division of attention, and proper planning.

B. TASK: POWER FAILURE AT ALTITUDE

REFERENCES: FAA-H-8083-21; POH/RFM.

NOTE: Simulated power failure at altitude shall be given over areas where actual touchdowns can safely be completed in the event of an actual powerplant failure.

Objective. To determine that the applicant:

1. Exhibits knowledge of the elements related to power failure at altitude.
2. Establishes an autorotation and selects a suitable landing area.
3. Establishes proper aircraft trim and autorotation airspeed, ±5 knots.
4. Maintains rotor RPM within normal limits.
5. Compensates for windspeed and direction as necessary to avoid undershooting or overshooting the selected landing area.
6. Terminates approach with a power recovery at a safe altitude when directed by the examiner.

C. TASK: SYSTEMS AND EQUIPMENT MALFUNCTIONS

REFERENCES: FAA-H-8083-21; POH/RFM.

Objective.   To determine that the applicant:

1. Exhibits knowledge of the elements related to causes, indications, and pilot actions for various systems and equipment malfunctions.
2. Analyzes the situation and takes action, appropriate to the helicopter used for the practical test, in at least three of the following areas—

   a. engine/oil and fuel.
   b. hydraulic, if applicable.
   c. electrical.
   d. carburetor or induction icing.
   e. smoke and/or fire.
   f. flight control/trim.
   g. pitot static/vacuum and associated flight instruments, if applicable.
   h. rotor and/or antitorque.
   i. various frequency vibrations and the possible components that may be affected.
   j. any other emergency unique to the helicopter flown.

D. TASK: SETTLING-WITH-POWER

REFERENCES: FAA-H-8083-21; POH/RFM.

Objective.   To determine that the applicant:

1. Exhibits knowledge of the elements related to settling-with-power.
2. Selects an altitude that will allow recovery to be completed no less than 1,000 feet AGL or, if applicable, the manufacturer's recommended altitude, whichever is higher.
3. Promptly recognizes and recovers at the onset of settling-with-power.
4. Utilizes the appropriate recovery procedure.

E. TASK: LOW ROTOR RPM RECOVERY

REFERENCES: FAA-H-8083-21; Appropriate Manufacturer's Safety Notices; POH/RFM.

NOTE: The examiner may test the applicant orally on this TASK if helicopter used for the practical test has a governor that cannot be disabled.

Objective. To determine that the applicant:

1. Exhibits knowledge of the elements related to low rotor RPM recovery, including the combination of conditions that are likely to lead to this situation.
2. Detects the development of low rotor RPM and initiates prompt corrective action.
3. Utilizes the appropriate recovery procedure.

F. TASK: ANTITORQUE SYSTEM FAILURE

REFERENCES: FAA-H-8083-21; POH/RFM.

Objective. To determine that the applicant:

1. Exhibits knowledge of the elements related to anit-torque system failure by describing:

    a. The aerodynamic indications of the types of possible system failure(s) associate with the helicopter.
    b. Manufacturers recommended procedures for dealing with the different types of system(s) failure

G. TASK: DYNAMIC ROLLOVER

REFERENCES: FAA-H-8083-21; POH/RFM.

Objective. To determine that the applicant:

1. Exhibits knowledge of the elements related to the aerodynamics of dynamic rollover.
2. Understands the interaction between the antitorque thrust, crosswind, slope, CG, cyclic, and collective pitch control in contributing to dynamic rollover.
3. Explains preventive flight technique during takeoffs, landings, and slope operations.

H. TASK: GROUND RESONANCE

REFERENCES: FAA-H-8083-21; POH/RFM.

Objective. To determine that the applicant:

1. Exhibits knowledge of the- elements related to a fully articulated rotor system and the aerodynamics of ground resonance.
2. Understands the conditions that contribute to ground resonance.
3. Explains preventive flight technique during takeoffs and landings.

I. TASK: LOW G CONDITIONS

REFERENCES: FAA-H-8083-21, POH/RFM.

Objective. To determine that the applicant:

1. Exhibits knowledge of the elements related to low G conditions.
2. Understands and recognizes the situations that contribute to low G conditions.
3. Explains proper recovery procedures.

J. TASK: EMERGENCY EQUIPMENT AND SURVIVAL GEAR

REFERENCES: FAA-H-8083-21; POH/RFM.

Objective. To determine that the applicant:

1. Exhibits knowledge of the elements related to emergency equipment and survival gear appropriate to the helicopter environment encountered during flight.
2. Identifies appropriate equipment that should be aboard the helicopter.

IX. AREA OF OPERATION: NIGHT OPERATION

A. TASK: NIGHT PREPARATION

REFERENCES: FAA-H-8083-21, FAA-H-8083-25; AIM; POH/AFM.

Objective. To determine that the applicant exhibits knowledge of the elements related to night operations by explaining:

1. Physiological aspects of night flying as it relates to vision.
2. Lighting systems identifying airports/helioports, runways, taxiways and obstructions, and pilot controlled lighting.
3. Helicopter lighting systems.
4. Personal equipment essential for night flight.
5. Night orientation, navigation, and chart reading techniques.
6. Safety precautions and emergencies unique to night flying.

X. AREA OF OPERATION: POST-FLIGHT PROCEDURES

A. TASK: AFTER LANDING AND SECURING

REFERENCES: FAA-H-8083-21; POH/RFM.

Objective. To determine that the applicant:

1. Exhibits knowledge of the elements related to after-landing, parking and securing procedures
2. Minimizes the hazardous effects of rotor downwash during hovering.
3. Parks in an appropriate area, considering the safety of nearby persons and property.
4. Follows the appropriate procedure for engine shutdown.
5. Completes the appropriate checklist.
6. Conducts an appropriate postflight inspection and secures the aircraft.

FAA-S-8081-15A

SECTION 2

PRIVATE PILOT
ROTORCRAFT – GYROPLANE

Practical Test Standards

CONTENTS: SECTION 2

Addition of a Rotorcraft/Gyroplane rating to an existing Private Pilot Certificate

Area of Opera-tion	Required TASKS are indicated by either the TASK letter(s) that apply(s) or an indication that all or none of the TASKS must be tested.								
	PRIVATE PILOT RATING(S) HELD								
	A SEL	AS ES	A MEL	A MES	R H	Non-Power Glider	Power Glider	Free Balloon	Airship
I	E,F,G	E,F,G	E,F,G	E,F,G	E,F,G	E,F,G,	E,F,G,	E,F,G,	E,F,G
II	ALL	ALL	ALL	ALL	ALL	ALL	ALL	ALL	ALL
III	B	B,C	B	B,C	B	ALL	B	ALL	B
IV	ALL	ALL	ALL	ALL	ALL	ALL	ALL	ALL	ALL
V	ALL	ALL	ALL	ALL	ALL	ALL	ALL	ALL	ALL
VI	ALL	ALL	ALL	ALL	ALL	ALL	ALL	ALL	ALL
VII	NONE	NONE	NONE	NONE	NONE	B,C,D	B,C,D	B,C,D	NONE
VIII	ALL	ALL	ALL	ALL	ALL	ALL	ALL	ALL	ALL
IX	ALL	ALL	ALL	ALL	ALL	ALL	ALL	ALL	ALL
X	NONE	NONE	NONE	NONE	NONE	ALL	ALL	ALL	ALL
XI	ALL	ALL	ALL	ALL	ALL	ALL	ALL	ALL	ALL

FAA-S-8081-15A

APPLICANT'S PRACTICAL TEST CHECKLIST
(GYROPLANE)
APPOINTMENT WITH EXAMINER:

EXAMINER'S NAME _____

LOCATION _____

DATE/TIME _____

ACCEPTABLE AIRCRAFT

Aircraft Documents:
   Airworthiness Certificate
   Registration Certificate
   Operating Limitations
Aircraft Maintenance Records:
   Logbook Record of Airworthiness Inspections
   and AD Compliance
Pilot's Operating Handbook, FAA-Approved
   Helicopter Flight Manual
FCC Station License

PERSONAL EQUIPMENT

Current Aeronautical Charts
Computer and Plotter
Flight Plan Form
Flight Logs
Current AIM, Airport Facility Directory, and Appropriate
   Publications

PERSONAL RECORDS

Identification - Photo/Signature ID
Pilot Certificate
Current and Appropriate Medical Certificate
Completed FAA Form 8710-1, Airman Certificate and/or
   Rating Application with Instructor's Signature (if
   applicable)
AC Form 8080-2, Airman Written Test Report, or
   Computer Test Report
Pilot Logbook with Appropriate Instructor Endorsements
FAA Form 8060-5, Notice of Disapproval (if applicable)
Approved School Graduation Certificate (if applicable)
Examiner's Fee (if applicable)

EXAMINER'S PRACTICAL TEST CHECKLIST

(GYROPLANE)

APPLICANT'S NAME _____

LOCATION _____

DATE/TIME _____

I. **PREFLIGHT PREPARATION**

    A. CERTIFICATES AND DOCUMENTS
    B. AIRWORTHINESS REQUIREMENTS
    C. WEATHER INFORMATION
    D. CROSS-COUNTRY FLIGHT PLANNING
    E. NATIONAL AIRSPACE SYSTEM
    F. PERFORMANCE AND LIMITATIONS
    G. OPERATION OF SYSTEMS
    H. AEROMEDICAL FACTORS

II. **PREFLIGHT PROCEDURES**

    A. PREFLIGHT INSPECTION
    B. COCKPIT MANAGEMENT
    C. ENGINE STARTING
    D. TAXIING
    E. BEFORE TAKEOFF CHECK

III. **AIRPORT OPERATIONS**

    A. RADIO COMMUNICATIONS AND ATC LIGHT SIGNALS
    B. TRAFFIC PATTERNS
    C. AIRPORT MARKINGS AND LIGHTING

IV. **TAKEOFFS, LANDINGS, AND GO-AROUNDS**

    A. NORMAL AND CROSSWIND TAKEOFF AND CLIMB
    B. NORMAL AND CROSSWIND APPROACH AND LANDING
    C. SOFT-FIELD TAKEOFF AND CLIMB
    D. SOFT-FIELD APPROACH AND LANDING
    E. SHORT-FIELD TAKEOFF AND CLIMB
    F. SHORT-FIELD APPROACH AND LANDING
    G. GO-AROUND

FAA-S-8081-15A

V. PERFORMANCE MANEUVER

    A. STEEP TURNS

VI. GROUND REFERENCE MANEUVERS

    A. RECTANGULAR COURSE
    B. S-TURNS
    C. TURNS AROUND A POINT

VII. NAVIGATION

    A. PILOTAGE AND DEAD RECKONING
    B. RADIO NAVIGATION AND RADAR SERVICES
    C. DIVERSION
    D. LOST PROCEDURES

VIII. FLIGHT AT SLOW AIRSPEEDS

    A. MANEUVERING AT SLOW AIRSPEEDS
    B. HIGH RATE OF DESCENT AND RECOVERY

IX. EMERGENCY OPERATIONS

    A. EMERGENCY APPROACH AND LANDING
    B. LIFT-OFF AT LOW AIRSPEED AND HIGH ANGLE OF ATTACK
    C. GROUND RESONANCE
    D. SYSTEMS AND EQUIPMENT MALFUNCTIONS
    E. EMERGENCY EQUIPMENT AND SURVIVAL GEAR

X. NIGHT OPERATIONS

    A. NIGHT PREPARATION

XI. POST-FLIGHT PROCEDURES

    A. AFTER LANDING, PARKING, AND SECURING

I. AREA OF OPERATION: PREFLIGHT PREPARATION

NOTE: The examiner shall develop a scenario based on real time weather to evaluate TASKs C, D, E, and F.

A. TASK: CERTIFICATES AND DOCUMENTS

REFERENCES: 14 CFR parts 43, 61, 67, 91; FAA-H-8083-21, FAA-H-8083-25; Gyroplane Flight Manual.

Objective. To determine that the applicant exhibits knowledge of the elements related to certificates and documents by:

1. Explaining—

    a. private pilot certificate privileges, limitations, and recent flight experience requirements.
    b. medical certificate class and duration.
    c. pilot logbook or flight records.

2. Locating and explaining—

    a. airworthiness and registration certificates.
    b. operating limitations, placards, instrument markings, and gyroplane flight manual.
    b. weight and balance data and equipment list.

B. TASK: AIRWORTHINESS REQUIREMENTS

REFERENCES: 14 CFR part 91; FAA-H-8083-21.

Objective. To determine that the applicant exhibits knowledge of the elements related to airworthiness requirements by:

1. Explaining—

    a. required instruments and equipment for day/night VFR.
    b. procedures and limitations for determining airworthiness of the gyroplane with inoperative instruments and equipment with and without an MEL.
    c. requirements and procedures for obtaining a special flight permit.

2. Locating and explaining—

    a. airworthiness directives.
    b. compliance records.
    c. maintenance/inspection requirements.
    d. appropriate record keeping.

C. TASK: WEATHER INFORMATION

REFERENCES: 14 CFR part 91; AC 00-6, AC 00-45, AC 61-84; FAA-H-8083-25; AIM.

Objective. To determine that the applicant:

1. Exhibits knowledge of the elements related to weather information by analyzing weather reports, charts, and forecasts from various sources with emphasis on—

   a. METAR, TAF, and FA.
   b. surface analysis chart.
   c. radar summary chart.
   d. winds and temperature aloft chart.
   e. significant weather prognostic charts.
   f. AWOS, ASOS, and ATIS reports.

2. Makes a competent "go/no-go" decision based on available weather information.

D. TASK: CROSS-COUNTRY FLIGHT PLANNING

REFERENCES: 14 CFR part 91; FAA-H-8083-25; AC 61-84; Navigation Charts; Airport/Facility Directory; NOTAMS; AIM.

Objective. To determine that the applicant:

1. Exhibits knowledge of the elements related to cross-country flight planning by presenting and explaining a pre-planned VFR cross-country flight, as previously assigned by the examiner. On the day of the practical test, the final flight plan shall be to the first fuel stop necessary, based on maximum allowable passengers, baggage, and/or cargo loads using real-time weather.
2. Uses appropriate and current aeronautical charts.
3 Properly identifies airspace, obstructions, and terrain features, including discussion of wire strike avoidance techniques.
4. Selects easily identifiable en route checkpoints.
5. Selects the most favorable altitudes, considering weather conditions and equipment capabilities.
6. Computes headings, flight time, and fuel requirements.
7. Selects appropriate navigation systems/facilities and communication frequencies.
8. Applies pertinent information from NOTAMs, AFD, and other flight publications.
9. Completes a navigation log and simulates filing a VFR flight plan.

E. TASK: NATIONAL AIRSPACE SYSTEM

REFERENCES: 14 CFR parts 71, 91; Navigation Charts; AIM.

Objective. To determine that the applicant exhibits knowledge of the elements related to the National Airspace System by explaining:

1. Basic VFR Weather Minimums – for all classes of airspace.
2. Airspace classes – their boundaries, pilot certification, and gyroplane equipment requirements for the following—

   a. Class A.
   b. Class B.
   c. Class C.
   d. Class D.
   e. Class E.
   f. Class G.

3. Special use airspace and other airspace areas.

F. TASK: PERFORMANCE AND LIMITATIONS

REFERENCES: FAA-H-8083-1, FAA-H-8083-21; AC 61-84; Gyroplane Flight Manual.

Objective. To determine that the applicant:

1. Exhibits knowledge of the elements related to performance and limitations by explaining the use of charts, tables, and data to determine performance and the adverse effects of exceeding limitations.
2. Computes weight and balance. Determines the computed weight and center of gravity is within the gyroplane's operating limitations and if the weight and center of gravity will remain within limits during all phases of flight.
3. Demonstrates the use of appropriate performance charts, tables, and data.
4. Describes the effects of atmospheric conditions on the gyroplane's performance.
5. Understands the cause, effect, and avoidance procedure of "power pushover," and "pilot induced oscillation."

G. TASK: OPERATION OF SYSTEMS

REFERENCES: FAA-H-8083-21; Gyroplane Flight Manual.

Objective.   To determine that the applicant exhibits knowledge of the elements related to the operation of systems on the gyroplane provided for the flight test by explaining at least three (3) of the following systems selected by the examiner.

1. Primary flight controls and trim.
2. Powerplant.
3. Rotor, including prerotator/spin-up control, if applicable.
4. Landing gear, brakes, and steering.
5. Fuel, oil, and hydraulic.
6. Electrical.
7. Pitot-static, vacuum/pressure, and associated flight instruments, if applicable.
8. Environmental, if applicable.
9. Anti-icing, including carburetor heat, if applicable.
10. Avionics equipment.

H. TASK: AEROMEDICAL FACTORS

REFERENCES: FAA-H-8083-21; AIM.

Objective.   To determine that the applicant exhibits knowledge of the elements related to aeromedical factors by explaining:

1. The symptoms, causes, effects, and corrective actions of at least three of the following—

   a. hypoxia.
   b. hyperventilation.
   c. middle ear and sinus problems.
   d. spatial disorientation.
   e. motion sickness.
   f. carbon monoxide poisoning.
   g. stress and fatigue.

2. The effects of alcohol and drugs, including over-the-counter drugs.
3. The effects of nitrogen excesses during scuba dives upon a pilot and/or passenger in flight.

II. AREA OF OPERATION: PREFLIGHT PROCEDURES

A. TASK: PREFLIGHT INSPECTION

REFERENCES: FAA-H-8083-21; Gyroplane Flight Manual.

Objective.   To determine that the applicant:

1. Exhibits knowledge of the elements related to a preflight inspection including which items must be inspected, the reasons for checking each item, and how to detect possible defects.
2. Inspects the gyroplane with reference to an appropriate checklist.
3. Verifies that the gyroplane is in condition for safe flight.

B. TASK: COCKPIT MANAGEMENT

REFERENCES: 14 CFR part 91; AC 91-32; FAA-H-8083-21; Gyroplane Flight Manual.

Objective.   To determine that the applicant:

1. Exhibits knowledge of the elements related to cockpit management procedures.
2. Ensures all loose items in the aircraft are secured.
3. Organizes and arranges material and equipment in an efficient manner so they are readily available.
4. Briefs the occupants on the use of safety belts, shoulder harnesses, doors, propeller and rotor blade avoidance, and emergency procedures.

C. TASK: ENGINE STARTING

REFERENCES: AC 91-13, AC 91-42, AC 91-55; FAA-H-8083-21, FAA-H-8083-25; Gyroplane Flight Manual.

Objective.   To determine that the applicant:

1. Exhibits knowledge of the elements related to recommended engine starting procedures. This shall include the use of an external power source, starting under various atmospheric conditions, awareness of other persons and property during start, and the effects of using incorrect starting procedures.
2. Positions the gyroplane properly considering structures, surface conditions, other aircraft, and the safety of nearby persons and property.
3. Utilizes the appropriate checklist for starting procedure.

D. TASK: TAXIING

REFERENCES: FAA-H-8083-21, FAA-H-8083-25; AIM; Gyroplane Flight Manual.

Objective. To determine that the applicant:

1. Exhibits knowledge of the elements related to recommended taxi procedures, including rotor blade management and the effect of wind during taxiing.
2. Performs a brake check immediately after the gyroplane begins moving.
3. Properly positions rotor blades while taxiing.
4. Controls direction and speed without excessive use of brakes.
5. Complies with airport markings, signals, ATC clearances, and instructions.
6. Avoids other aircraft and hazards.
7. Properly positions the gyroplane for runup considering other aircraft, surface conditions, and if applicable, existing wind conditions.

E. TASK: BEFORE TAKEOFF CHECK

REFERENCES: FAA-H-8083-21, FAA-H-8083-25; Gyroplane Flight Manual.

Objective. To determine that the applicant:

1. Exhibits knowledge of the elements related to the before takeoff check. This shall include the reasons for checking the items and how to detect malfunctions.
2. Positions the gyroplane properly considering other aircraft, surface conditions, and wind conditions.
3. Divides attention inside and outside the aircraft.
4. Accomplishes the before takeoff check and ensures that the gyroplane is in safe operating condition.
5. Reviews takeoff performance airspeeds and expected takeoff distance.
6. Describes takeoff emergency procedures, to include low speed/ high speed blade flap situations.
7. Avoids runway incursions and/or ensures no conflict with traffic prior to taxiing into takeoff position.
8. Utilizes proper rotor spin-up procedure.

III. AREA OF OPERATION: AIRPORT OPERATIONS

A. TASK: RADIO COMMUNICATIONS AND ATC LIGHT SIGNALS

REFERENCES: 14 CFR part 91; FAA-H-8083-25; AIM.

Objective. To determine that the applicant:

1. Exhibits knowledge of the elements related to radio communications and ATC light signals.
2. Selects appropriate frequencies.
3. Transmits using recommended phraseology.
4. Acknowledges radio communications and complies with instructions.

B. TASK: TRAFFIC PATTERNS

REFERENCES: 14 CFR part 91; AIM; Gyroplane Flight Manual.

Objective. To determine that the applicant:

1. Exhibits knowledge of the elements related to traffic patterns. This shall include procedures at airports with and without operating control towers, prevention of runway incursions, collision avoidance, wake turbulence avoidance, and wind shear.
2. Complies with proper traffic pattern procedures.
3. Maintains proper spacing from other traffic.
4. Corrects for wind drift to maintain the proper ground track.
5. Maintains orientation with the runway/landing area in use.
6. Maintains traffic pattern altitude, ±100 feet, and the appropriate airspeed, ±5 knots.

C. TASK: AIRPORT MARKINGS AND LIGHTING

REFERENCES: FAA-H-8083-25; AIM.

Objective.   To determine that the applicant:

1. Exhibits knowledge of the elements related to airport runway and taxiway operations with emphasis on runway incursion avoidance.
2. Properly identifies and interprets airport runway and taxiway signs, markings, and lighting.

IV. AREA OF OPERATION: TAKEOFFS, LANDINGS, AND GO-AROUNDS

NOTE: If the gyroplane provided for the test is not capable of safely performing soft field or short field maneuvers the applicant may be tested orally on their knowledge of the basic procedures.

A. TASK: NORMAL AND CROSSWIND TAKEOFF AND CLIMB

REFERENCES: FAA-H-8083-21; Gyroplane Flight Manual.

NOTE: If a crosswind condition does not exist, the applicant's knowledge of crosswind elements shall be evaluated through oral testing.

Objective. To determine that the applicant:

1. Exhibits knowledge of the elements related to a normal and crosswind takeoff, climb operations, and rejected takeoff procedures. Positions the flight controls for the existing wind conditions.
2. Prerotates rotor blades to appropriate RPM.
3. Clears the area, taxies into the takeoff position, and aligns the gyroplane with takeoff path.
4. Advances the throttle as required.
5. Maintains proper directional control during acceleration on the surface.
6. Attains the proper lift-off attitude, and airspeed.
7. Accelerates to appropriate climb airspeed, ±5 knots.
8. Maintains takeoff power to a safe maneuvering altitude, then sets climb power.
9. Maintains directional control and proper wind-drift correction throughout the takeoff and climb.
10. Remains aware of the possibility of wind shear and/or wake turbulence.
11. Completes the prescribed checklist, if applicable.

B. TASK: NORMAL AND CROSSWIND APPROACH AND LANDING

REFERENCES: FAA-H-8083-21; Gyroplane Flight Manual.

NOTE: If a crosswind condition does not exist, the applicant's knowledge of crosswind elements shall be evaluated through oral testing.

Objective. To determine that the applicant:

1. Exhibits knowledge of the elements related to normal and crosswind approach and landing.
2. Adequately surveys the intended landing area.
3. Considers the wind conditions, landing surface, obstructions, and selects a suitable touchdown point.
4. Establishes and maintains a stabilized approach at the recommended airspeed, with gust correction factor applied, ±5 knots.
5. Maintains proper ground track with crosswind correction, if necessary.
6. Remains aware of the possibility of wind shear and/or wake turbulence.
7. Makes smooth, timely, and correct control application during the flare and touchdown
8. Touches down smoothly, beyond and within 200 feet of a specified point with no appreciable drift, and with the longitudinal axis aligned with the intended landing path.
9. Completes the appropriate checklist.

C. TASK: SOFT-FIELD TAKEOFF AND CLIMB

REFERENCES: FAA-H-8083-21; Gyroplane Flight Manual.

Objective. To determine that the applicant:

1. Exhibits knowledge of the elements related to a soft-field takeoff and climb.
2. Determines and utilizes best takeoff procedure based on the capabilities of this gyroplane and current conditions.
3. Positions the flight controls for existing wind conditions and to maximize lift as quickly as possible.
4. Prerotates rotor blades to appropriate RPM.
5. Clears the area; taxies onto the takeoff surface at a speed consistent with safety, without stopping, while advancing the throttle smoothly to takeoff power.
6. Maintains proper directional control.
7. Lifts off and remains in ground effect while accelerating to recommended climb airspeed.
8. Maintains recommended climb airspeed, ±5 knots.
9. Maintains takeoff power to a safe maneuvering altitude, then sets climb power.
10. Maintains proper ground track with crosswind correction, if necessary.
11. Remains aware of the possibility of wind shear and/or wake turbulence.
12. Completes the appropriate checklist.

D. TASK: SOFT-FIELD APPROACH AND LANDING

REFERENCES: FAA-H-8083-21; Gyroplane Flight Manual.

Objective. To determine that the applicant:

1. Exhibits knowledge of the elements related to a soft-field approach and landing.
2. Considers the wind conditions, landing surface, and obstacles, and selects the most suitable touchdown area.
3. Establishes and maintains a stabilized approach at the recommended airspeed, with gust correction factor applied, ±5 knots.
4. Maintains proper ground track with crosswind correction, if necessary.
5. Remains aware of the possibility of wind shear and/or wake turbulence.
6. Makes smooth, timely, and correct control application during the flare and touchdown.
7. Touches down smoothly, at a minimum descent rate and airspeed with no appreciable drift, and with the longitudinal axis aligned with the intended landing path.
8. Completes the appropriate checklist

E. TASK: SHORT-FIELD TAKEOFF AND CLIMB

REFERENCES: FAA-H-8083-21; Gyroplane Flight Manual.

Objective.   To determine that the applicant:

1. Exhibits knowledge of the elements related to short-field takeoff and maximum performance climb
2. Properly positions controls.
3. Prerotates rotor blades to appropriate RPM.
4. Clears the area, taxies into the takeoff position and aligns the gyroplane for maximum utilization of available takeoff area.
5. Advances the throttle as required.
6. Climbs at manufacturer's recommended airspeed, or in its absence at V_x, ±5 knots until the obstacle is cleared, or until the gyroplane is at least 50 feet above the surface.
7. After clearing the obstacle, accelerates to appropriate airspeed, ±5 knots.
8. Maintains takeoff power to a safe maneuvering altitude, then sets climb power.
9. Maintains directional control and proper wind-drift correction throughout the takeoff and climb.
10. Remains aware of the possibility of wind shear and/or wake turbulence.
11. Completes the appropriate checklist.

F. TASK: SHORT-FIELD APPROACH AND LANDING

REFERENCES: FAA-H-8083-21; Gyroplane Flight Manual.

Objective. To determine that the applicant:

1. Exhibits knowledge of the elements related to short-field approach and landing.
2. Considers the wind conditions, landing surface, and obstacles.
3. Selects a suitable touchdown point.
4. Establishes and maintains a stabilized approach at the recommended airspeed, with gust correction factor applied, ±5 knots.
5. Maintains proper ground track with crosswind correction, if necessary.
6. Remains aware of the possibility of wind shear and/or wake turbulence.
7. Makes smooth, timely, and correct control application during the flare and touchdown.
8. Touches down smoothly, with little or no float beyond and within 100 feet of a specified point with no appreciable drift, and with the longitudinal axis aligned with the intended landing path.
9. Applies brakes, as necessary, to stop in the shortest distance consistent with safety.
10. Completes the prescribed checklist, if applicable.

G. TASK: GO-AROUND

REFERENCES: FAA-H-8083-21; Gyroplane Flight Manual.

Objective. To determine that the applicant:

1. Exhibits knowledge of the elements related to a go-around and when it is necessary.
2. Makes a timely decision to discontinue the approach to landing.
3. Applies appropriate power and establishes a climb at the appropriate airspeed, ±5 knots.
4. Maintains takeoff power to a safe maneuvering altitude, then sets climb power.
5. Maintains proper ground track with crosswind correction, if necessary.
6. Completes the prescribed checklist, if applicable.

V. AREA OF OPERATION: PERFORMANCE MANEUVER

TASK: STEEP TURNS

REFERENCES: FAA-H-8083-21; Gyroplane Flight Manual.

Objective.   To determine that the applicant:

1. Exhibits knowledge of the elements related to steep turns.
2. Selects a safe altitude.
3. Establishes the manufacturer's recommended airspeed or if one is not stated, a safe airspeed not to exceed V_A.
4. Smoothly enters a coordinated steep 360° turn with a 40° bank.
5. Performs the task in the opposite direction, as specified by the examiner.
6. Divides attention between gyroplane control and orientation.
7. Maintains the entry altitude, ±100 feet, airspeed, ±10 knots, bank, ±5°; and rolls out on the entry heading, ±10°.

VI. AREA OF OPERATION: GROUND REFERENCE MANEUVERS

NOTE: The examiner shall select at least one TASK.

A. TASK: RECTANGULAR COURSE

REFERENCE: FAA-H-8083-21.

Objective.   To determine that the applicant:

1. Exhibits knowledge of the elements related to a rectangular course.
2. Selects an appropriate ground reference based on wind direction and emergency landing areas.
3. Plans the maneuver so as to enter a left or right pattern, 600 to 1,000 feet AGL (180 to 300 meters) at an appropriate distance from the selected reference area, 45° to the downwind leg.
4. Applies adequate wind-drift correction during straight-and-turning flight to maintain a constant ground track around the rectangular reference area.
5. Divides attention between gyroplane control and the ground track while maintaining coordinated flight.
6. Maintains altitude, ±100 feet; maintains airspeed, ±10 knots.

B. TASK: S-TURNS

REFERENCE: FAA-H-8083-21.

Objective.   To determine that the applicant:

1. Exhibits knowledge of the elements related to S-turns.
2. Selects an appropriate reference line based on wind direction and emergency landing areas.
3. Plans the maneuver so as to enter at 600 to 1,000 feet (180 to 300 meters) AGL, perpendicular to the selected reference line.
4. Applies adequate wind-drift correction to track a constant radius turn on each side of the selected reference line.
5. Reverses the direction of turn directly over the selected reference line.
6. Divides attention between gyroplane control and the ground track while maintaining coordinated flight.
7. Maintains the entry altitude throughout the maneuver, ±100 feet; maintains airspeed, ±10 knots.

C. TASK: TURNS AROUND A POINT

REFERENCE: FAA-H-8083-21.

Objective. To determine that the applicant:

1. Exhibits knowledge of the elements related to turns around a point.
2. Selects an appropriate reference point based on wind direction and emergency landing areas.
3. Plans the maneuver so as to enter left or right at 600 to 1,000 feet (180 to 300 meters) AGL, at an appropriate distance from the reference point.
4. Applies adequate wind-drift correction to track a constant radius circle around the selected reference point with a bank of approximately 40° at the steepest point in the turn.
5. Divides attention between gyroplane control and the ground track while maintaining coordinated flight.
6. Maintains altitude, ±100 feet; maintains airspeed, ±10 knots.

VII. AREA OF OPERATION: NAVIGATION

A. TASK: PILOTAGE AND DEAD RECKONING

REFERENCES: FAA-H-8083-25; AC 61-84.

Objective.   To determine that the applicant:

1. Exhibits knowledge of the elements related to pilotage and dead reckoning.
2. Correctly flies to at least the first planned checkpoint to demonstrate accuracy in computations.
3. Identifies landmarks by relating surface features to chart symbols.
4. Navigates by means of precomputed headings, groundspeed, and elapsed time.
5. Verifies the gyroplane's position within 3 nautical miles of the flight planned route at all times.
6. Arrives at the en route checkpoints within 5 minutes of the initial or revised ETA and provides a destination estimate.
7. Maintains the appropriate altitude, ±200 feet and established heading, ±15°.

B. TASK: NAVIGATION AND RADAR SERVICES

REFERENCES: FAA-H-8083-25; AC 61-84; Navigation Equipment Operation Manuals.

NOTE: If the gyroplane is not equipped with electronic navigation aids, competency will be evaluated through oral testing.

Objective.   To determine that the applicant:

1. Exhibits knowledge of the elements related to navigation and ATC radar services.
2. Demonstrates the ability to use an airborne electronic navigation system.
3. Locates the gyroplane's position using the navigation system.
4. Intercepts and tracks a given course radial or bearing, as appropriate.
5. Recognizes and describes the indication of station or waypoint passage, if appropriate.
6 Recognizes signal loss and takes appropriate action.
7. Uses proper communication procedures when utilizing ATC radar services.
8. Maintains the appropriate altitude, ±200 feet and headings, ±15°.

C. TASK: DIVERSION

REFERENCES: FAA-H-8083-25; AC 61-84.

Objective.   To determine that the applicant:

1. Exhibits knowledge of the elements related to diversion.
2. Selects an appropriate alternate airport and route.
3. Makes an accurate estimate of heading, groundspeed, arrival time, and fuel consumption to the alternate airport.
4. Maintains the appropriate altitude, ±200 feet and established heading, ±15°.

D. TASK: LOST PROCEDURES

REFERENCES: FAA-H-8083-25; AC 61-84; AIM.

Objective.   To determine that the applicant:

1. Exhibits knowledge of the elements related to lost procedures.
2. Selects an appropriate course of action.
3. Maintains an appropriate heading, and climbs if necessary.
4. Identifies prominent landmarks.
5. Uses available navigation aids and/or contacts an appropriate facility for assistance, if gyroplane is radio equipped.
6. Plans a precautionary landing if deteriorating weather and/or fuel exhaustion is impending.

VIII. AREA OF OPERATION: FLIGHT AT SLOW AIRSPEEDS

A. TASK: MANEUVERING AT SLOW AIRSPEEDS

REFERENCES: FAA-H-8083-21; Gyroplane Flight Manual.

Objective.   To determine that the applicant:

1. Exhibits knowledge of the elements related to flight characteristics and controllability associated with maneuvering during slow flight.
2. Selects a safe altitude.
3. Establishes and maintains a specified airspeed +5, -0, in straight-and-level flight, turns, climbs, and descents as directed.
4. Maintains the specified altitude, ±100 feet.
5. Maintains the specified heading during straight flight, ±10°.
6. Maintains specified bank angle, ±10°, during turning flight.
7. Rolls out on specified headings, ±10°.
8. Divides attention between gyroplane control and orientation.

B. TASK: HIGH RATE OF DESCENT AND RECOVERY

REFERENCES: FAA-H-8083-21; Gyroplane Flight Manual.

Objective.   To determine that the applicant:

1. Exhibits knowledge of the elements related to aerodynamic factors associated with a high rate of descent and recovery and how this relates to actual approach and landing situations.
2. Selects an entry altitude that allows the task to be completed no lower than 500 feet AGL.
3. Establishes an airspeed that will induce a high rate of descent in high or low power settings.
4. Recognizes the onset of a high rate of descent.
5. Promptly recovers with or without power as directed.
6. Maintains the specified heading, ±10°.
7. Resumes normal cruising flight.

IX. AREA OF OPERATION: EMERGENCY OPERATIONS

NOTE: TASK B may be tested orally at the discretion of the examiner. TASKs C through E are knowledge only items.

A. TASK: EMERGENCY APPROACH AND LANDING

REFERENCES: FAA-H-8083-21; Gyroplane Flight Manual.

Objective.   To determine that the applicant:

1. Exhibits knowledge of the elements related to emergency approach and landing with a power failure.
2. Establishes and maintains the appropriate airspeed, ±5 knots.
3. Selects a suitable landing area, considering the possibility of an actual forced landing.
4. Plans and follows a flight pattern to the selected landing area, considering altitude, wind, terrain, obstacles, and other factors.
5. Attempts to determine the reason for the simulated malfunction, if time permits.
6. Completes the prescribed checklist, if applicable.

B. TASK: LIFT-OFF AT LOW AIRSPEED AND HIGH ANGLE OF ATTACK

REFERENCE: Gyroplane Flight Manual.

Objective.   To determine that the applicant:

1. Exhibits knowledge of the elements related to lift-off at low airspeed and high angle of attack, including combination of conditions, which are likely to lead to this situation.
2. Properly positions the controls.
3. Prerotates rotor blades to appropriate RPM, if applicable.
4. Clears the area; taxies into the takeoff position and aligns the gyroplane with the takeoff path.
5. Maintains proper directional control during acceleration on the surface.
6. Rotates for takeoff prior to normal lift-off airspeed with high angle of attack.
7. Detects the development of a low airspeed and high angle of attack, and initiates prompt corrective action.
8. Accelerates to recommended climb airspeed, ±5 knots.

C. TASK: GROUND RESONANCE

REFERENCES: FAA-H-8083-21; Gyroplane Flight Manual.

Objective. To determine that the applicant:

1. Exhibits knowledge of the elements related to a fully articulated rotor system and the aerodynamics of ground resonance.
2. Understands the conditions that contribute to ground resonance.
3. Explains preventive flight techniques used during takeoffs and landings.

D. TASK: SYSTEMS AND EQUIPMENT MALFUNCTIONS

REFERENCE: Gyroplane Flight Manual.

Objective. To determine that the applicant:

1. Exhibits knowledge of the elements related to causes, indications, and pilot actions for various systems and equipment malfunctions.
2. Analyzes the situation and takes action, appropriate to the gyroplane used for the practical test, in at least three of the following areas—

   a. engine/oil and fuel.
   b. hydraulic, if applicable.
   c. electrical.
   d. carburetor or induction icing.
   e. smoke and/or fire.
   f. flight control/trim.
   g. pitot static/vacuum and associated flight instruments, if applicable.
   h. rotor and/or propeller.
   i. any other emergency unique to the gyroplane flown.

E. TASK: EMERGENCY EQUIPMENT AND SURVIVAL GEAR

REFERENCES: FAA-H-8083-21; Gyroplane Flight Manual.

Objective. To determine that the applicant:

1. Exhibits knowledge of the elements related to emergency equipment and survival gear appropriate to the gyroplane and environment encountered during flight. Identifies appropriate equipment that should be aboard the gyroplane.

X. AREA OF OPERATION: NIGHT OPERATION

A. TASK: NIGHT PREPARATION

REFERENCES: FAA-H-8083-21, FAA-H-8083-25; AIM, Gyroplane Flight Manual.

Objective. To determine that the applicant exhibits knowledge of the elements related to night operations by explaining:

1. Physiological aspects of night flying as it relates to vision.
2. Lighting systems identifying airports, runways, taxiways and obstructions, and pilot controlled lighting.
3. Airplane lighting systems.
4. Personal equipment essential for night flight.
5. Night orientation, navigation, and chart reading techniques. Safety precautions and emergencies unique to night flying.

XI. AREA OF OPERATION: POST-FLIGHT PROCEDURES

A. TASK: AFTER LANDING, PARKING, AND SECURING

REFERENCES: FAA-H-8083-21, FAA-H-8083-25; AIM; Gyroplane Flight Manual.

Objective.   To determine that the applicant:

1. Exhibits knowledge of the elements related to after landing, parking and securing procedures.
2. Maintains directional control after touchdown while decelerating to an appropriate speed.
3. Observes runway hold lines and other surface control markings and lighting.
4. Parks in an appropriate area, considering the safety of nearby persons and property.
5. Follows the appropriate procedure for engine shutdown.
6. Completes the appropriate checklist.
7. Conducts an appropriate post flight inspection and secures the aircraft.

UPDATES TO THIS BOOK ARE FREE

www.cfidarren.com/register.htm

Protect your investment and register so that you can receive free publication updates, monthly newsletters, aviation safety notices, and free video training.

"Real knowledge is to know the extent of one's ignorance."

— *Confucius*

Aviation Safety Appendix

Topics
Personal Minimums Checklist
Metric Conversion Factors
Forms
Training Programs
Flight Gear
Publications

Personal Minimums Checklist

ADAPTATION REPRINT OF FAA P-8740-55 AFS-810(1996)

PILOT
AIRCRAFT
EN**V**IRONMENT
EXTERNAL
PRESSURES

Your Personal Minimums Checklist
O An easy-to-use, personal tool, tailored to your level of skill, knowledge & ability.
O Helps you control and manage risk by identifying even subtle risk factors
O Lets you fly with less stress and less risk.

Practice "Conservatism Without Guilt"
Each item provides you with either a space to complete a personal minimum or a checklist item to think about. Spend some quiet time completing each blank & consider other items that apply to your personal minimums. Give yourself permission to choose higher minimums than those specified in the regulations, aircraft flight manuals, or other rules.

How to Use Your Checklist
Use this checklist just as you would one for your aircraft. Carry the checklist in your flight kit. Use it at home as you start planning a flight and again just before you make your final decision to fly. Photocopy the next page (front & back) and carry extras in your flight bag. Be wary if you have an item that's marginal in any single risk factor category. But if you have items in more than one category, you may be headed for trouble.

If you have marginal items in two or more risk factors/categories, don't go!
Periodically review and revise your personal minimums checklist as your personal circumstances change, such as your proficiency, recency, or training. You should never make your minimums less restrictive unless a significant positive event has occurred. However, it is okay to make your minimums more restrictive at any time. Never make your minimums less restrictive when you are planning a specific flight, or else external pressures will influence you.

PILOT

Experience/Recency

Takeoffs/Landings   ____In the last ____days

Hours in make/model   ____In the last ____days

Instrument approaches   ____In the last
(simulated or actual)   ____days

Instrument flight hours   ____In the last
(simulated or actual)   ____days

Terrain and airspace   ____Familiar?

Physical Condition

Illnesses, none in the last   ____days

Medication/Drugs, none in ____days

Stressful Event, none in   ____days

Alcohol, none in the last   ____In the last 24hrs

Fatigue: hours of sleep   ____In the last 24hrs

Eating/Nourishment/Water ____hours ago

_____

_____

_____

_____

Thanks to:

FAA Aviation Safety Program
The Ohio State University
King Schools

AIRCRAFT

Fuel Reserves

VFR Day ____hours

Night ____hours

IFR Day ____hours

Night ____hours

Experience in type

Takeoffs/Landings ____In the last

(in aircraft type) ____days

Aircraft Performance

Consider the following:

- Gross weight ____
- Load distribution ____
- Density Altitude ____
- Performance Charts ____

Ensure you have a margin of safety

Aircraft Equipment

Avionics/GPS, familiar with ____

Autopilot, familiar with ____

COM/NAV, appropriate ____

Charts, current & adequate ____

Clothing, suitable for flight ____

Survival gear, suitable for flight ____

Required Documents (ARROW) ____

Required Inspections (AVIATE) ____

Required Equipment (§91.205) ____

Other ____

_____

_____

_____

_____

_____

EN**V**IRONMENT

Airport Conditions

Crosswind, Departure	_____	% max POH
Crosswind, Arrival	_____	% max POH
Runway length, Departure	_____	% over POH
Runway length, Arrival	_____	% over POH

Weather

Forecast, not more than	_____	Hours old
Icing conditions, familiar	_____	

Weather for VFR

Ceiling	Day	_____	feet
	Night	_____	feet
Visibility	Day	_____	miles
	Night	_____	miles

Weather for IFR

Precision Approaches

Ceiling	_____	ft above min
Visibility	_____	mi above min

Non-Precision Approaches

Ceiling	_____	ft above min
Visibility	_____	mi above min

Missed Approaches

No more than	_____	before divert

Takeoff Minimums

Ceiling	_____	feet
Visibility	_____	miles

_____

_____

_____

_____

_____

_____

EXTERNAL PRESSURES

Trip Planning
Allowance for delays, _____ minutes

Diversion/Cancellation Alternate Plans
✓ Notification of person(s) you are meeting.
✓ Passengers briefed on diversion/cancellation plans and alternates.
✓ Modification or cancellation of car rental, restaurant, or hotel reservations.
✓ Alternate transportation (air/car/etc)

Personal Equipment
✓ Credit card & telephone numbers available for alternate plans.
✓ Appropriate clothing or personal needs (eyewear, medication…) in the event of unexpected stay.

Importance of Trip
The more important the trip, the more tendency there is to compromise your personal minimums, and the more important it becomes to have alternate plans.

For More Information, Contact:

Darren Smith, ATP, CFII/MEI
Certificated Flight Instructor
www.cfidarren.com

Appendix B: Metric Conversion Tables

When you know:	Multiply by:	To find:	Length and Distance
inches (in)	2.54	centimeters	
feet (ft)	30.480	centimeters	
yards	.9144	meters (m)	
meters (m)	1.094	yards	
statute miles	.8684	nautical miles	
nautical miles	1.1516	statute miles	
statute miles	1.609	kilometers	
kilometers (km)	0.6213	statute miles	
miles/hour	88	feet/minute	

When you know:	Multiply by:	To find:	Volume and capacity (liquid)
gallons, US	3.785	liters	
liters (L)	0.2642	gallons, US	
gallons, Imp	4.546	liters	
liters (L)	0.22	gallons, Imp	

When you know:	Multiply by:	To find:	Weight and mass
ounces (oz)	28.350	grams	
pounds (lb)	0.4536	kilograms	
grams (g)	0.03527	ounces	
kilograms	2.205	pounds	

When you know:	Formula:	To find:	Temperature
°C	9/5°C+32	°F	
°F	5/9(°F-32)	°C	

Flight Operations Threat Analysis

A great way to avoid threat and resist error is performing a briefing. Briefings can bring an added element of safety to your flight by reviewing the threats for your flight, your takeoff, your approach, etc. Pilots who perform quality briefings, even single pilot, exhibit active leadership, airmanship, and professionalism. Much has been written in these pages about Threat & Error Management. This article introduces a tool you can use on every flight. The FOTA briefing.

The Flight Operations Threat Analysis (FOTA) briefing analyzes the threats facing the flight so that pilots can perform active avoidance of potential problems that can occur during a flight. You learned from the Threat & Error Management model that if you avoid the threat, it usually doesn't occur. Your avoidance activities will go a long way to minimizing a threat even if it does occur and results in easier threat management. If your threat management is successful, then the error is resisted and prevented.

An active Threat & Error Management mindset is required for today's complex operating environment. The FOTA briefing model used for every flight will go a long way to bringing an "airline level of safety" to your flying.

The briefing items include:

Security: any security related concerns, TFRs, etc.

Weather: departure, enroute, and arrival weather conditions were reviewed during your flight planning. The high points are covered here. Any items from your Personal Minimums Checklist which are at your limits should be included also.

Airport: conditions such as runway/LZ slope, size, type, and condition were reviewed during your preflight planning. Concerns should be listed here along with any parameter near its limits. For example wind conditions may be at or near your maximum demonstrated crosswind limitations for your aircraft.

Pilot: your experience considering the parameters of your flight, including recency, and any items from your Personal Minimums Checklist which are at your limits should be included also.

Aircraft: any airworthiness issues, inoperative equipment should be listed. Any performance considerations from your preflight planning should also be listed (i.e. take-off and landing charts, etc).

Flight Plan: any concerns in your fuel plan, altitudes in use, enroute emergency plans, and time available for the flight should be considered and listed.

Other: any other considerations that affect the safety of your flight should be listed.

There is a blank form in the back of this book that you can photocopy to use for your briefing purposes.

To the right is a sample form.

See the end of the book for some blank forms you can photocopy for your flights.

Flight Ops Threat Analysis

Security	No concerns
Weather	- Low IFR expected 1 hour after scheduled arrival. - Thunderstorms south of course.
Airport	Arrival: taxiway F closed
Pilot	Low IFR experience > 1 year ago.
Aircraft	ADF in-op
Flight Plan	No concerns
Other	FBO closed at alternate at ETA

Flight Operations Threat Analysis

Briefing form for Threats to Flight Safety

Security

Weather

Airport

Pilot

Aircraft

Flight Plan

Other

7-Day Instrument Rating Training

Structured, Efficient, & Cost Effective:

○ Get 7 days of <u>individualized experience</u> for Your Training Investment.
○ <u>Gain real confidence</u> working the IFR system with airline style routes.
○ <u>Learn real world techniques</u> from an experienced Instructor (CFII)
○ Build IFR skills in your aircraft - in a format convenient to your schedule.

Want to finish your IFR Rating in 7 days?

If you're interested in getting your instrument in 7 days, this is the program for you. There are no gimmicks to this, it's hard work, and requires your full concentration. But when you're finished, you'll have gained solid experience in the real world of IFR.

Don't spend 9-12 months and $7,000 to $10,000 on your instrument rating! Condensed training experiences will not only save you money, but the intensity guarantees that the lessons last a lifetime. Your training is accelerated and less time is spent reviewing the last lesson... a real money saver. None of the other accelerated programs provide the comprehensive, high quality learning materials: the Oral Exam Prep Kit and the Instrument Rating Checkride Reviewer.

The three-day IFR Adventure is an integral part of the seven day IFR Rating and guarantees a unique training experience. We integrate the IFR Adventure into the course not only to meet certain instrument rating requirements, but also to serve as a real world capstone experience which increases your confidence in the IFR system.

What if you want a slower pace than a 7 day instrument rating training course? A 10-day program is available at a slightly higher cost.

Key Features:

○ The program includes up to 56 hours of one-on-one ground & flight instruction.
○ You will receive <u>at least</u> 30 hours of one-on-one flight instruction on some of the most challenging instrument approaches in the South East. You'll fly at least 25 approaches during the program, many with SID's STAR's and holding patterns. You'll be astonished at how much you will learn.
○ When you are not in the air, you will learn techniques that will simplify otherwise complex procedures such as procedure turns, holding pattern entries and many others.
○ Includes a 3 day IFR Adventure which adds up to a true flying adventure that will make you a more knowledgeable and confident pilot... plus it's a whole lot of fun!
○ You are PIC for the entire program receiving PIC credit in your logbook for 100% of the flight time.
○ We know your aircraft—we've got time virtually all aircraft & helicopters and avionics configurations.

6 Reasons to Choose This Program:

1. This is a quick, efficient, structured training program to get you through this training with minimum pain, maximum quality.
2. We constantly evaluate our competitors to ensure that our program provides the highest quality at the most reasonable cost in the country... compare for yourself. We're not beat by anyone.
3. You are PIC for the entire program receiving PIC credit in your logbook for 100% of the flight time.
4. Safety: techniques for safe instrument flight are emphasized by your instructor.
5. Personal attention is provided as you progress through your training program. You'll never wonder about your progress. You will never fall through the cracks .
6. The chief instructor has been a teacher since 1996, is a Master Instructor (NAFI), Advanced Ground Instructor rated (FAA), a Gold Seal Certificated Flight Instructor (FAA), an Aviation Safety Counselor (FAA), and a former airline pilot. Your instructor is a highly qualified ATP-rated, FAA Gold Seal, NAFI Master instructor with 100% pass rate. None of the other local providers use an instructor of this calibre.

Prerequisites for Instrument Rating:

You'll be ready for a checkride immediately upon completion if you have:
○ a passing score on your instrument written,
○ at least 50 hours PIC X/C & at least 40 hours of instrument time,
○ and meet PTS requirements

Those that don't meet these requirements will receive instruction at reduced rate. This can be completed before or after the trip. What if you want a slower pace than a 7 day instrument rating training course? A 10-day program is available at a slightly higher cost.

Availability:

Call for scheduling.   Includes: All flight and ground instruction, over 56 hours combined. Orientation ground package.

Not Included: Aircraft or anything related to the aircraft (Fuel, Oil, Insurance, Rental, Gov Fees, Repair, Etc), Meals, Ground Transportation & Lodging for you & your instructor, entertainment or any personal expenses you might encounter. You must supply your own aircraft, oil & fuel.

Participant Comments:

"You have a 'teaching way' about you and its very effective." Dave C
"You really have this down to a science." Alan D
"Thank you for the many flights of stressing good flying habits.
Its now paying off in my Air Force career." Mark S
"My training was second to none. My skills are consistently
complimented by other flight instructors I have flown with" Tim N

www.ifrnow.com

South East IFR Adventure

In Your Aircraft

Our Practice Area is a 2,000 mile Cross
Country Training Adventure!

Intense 3-day IFR Confidence Builder

○ Get More Individualized Experience For Your Training Investment.
○ Gain real confidence working the IFR system with airline style routes.
○ Learn Real World Techniques from an experienced Instructor (CFII)
○ Finish your instrument rating or IPC & build IFR skills in your aircraft.
○ We can start your IFR adventure anyplace and customize it to your location.
○ Get more than current, get <u>proficient</u>.

Want a real IFR workout?

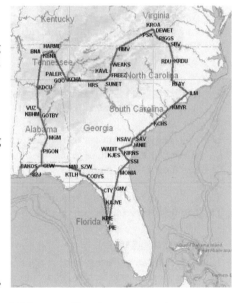

If you're interested in finishing
your instrument rating or gaining
solid experience in the real world
of IFR, here's a unique opportu-
nity for an accelerated program
for aircraft owners that is completed in **3 days**.

This Southeast Trip is a flying
adventure, traveling up the east
coast, down the Blue Ridge
Mountain chain to the Great
Smoky Mountain, through the
heartland, and back down
through the Mississippi Valley.
You will gain the experience of
flying over 2,000 miles and over
20 flight hours. Upon our return,
you'll receive your IPC or en-
dorsement for the check-ride. In addition, you'll enjoy spectacular scenery,
gain valuable experience by training away from your local airport and receive professional instruction in a variety of flight conditions.

This training experience gives you the confidence you need to really
use the IFR system. You'll operate in the environment like a professional
by focusing on the practical aspects of instrument flight. You will also get
a chance to really learn some of the most challenging instrument approaches in the country, performing them like the professionals.

Key Features:

O Your orientation includes ground instruction, briefings, flight planning.
O You will receive over 20 hours of one-on-one flight instruction on some of the most challenging instrument approaches in the Southeast.
O When you are not in the air, you will learn techniques that will simplify otherwise complex procedures such as procedure turns, holding pattern entries and many others.
O You'll receive over 10 hours of ground instruction during the course of the program... you will be confident you can pass your checkride.
O If instrument rated, you will receive your IPC immediately upon return. Instrument rating completion students will typically take their instrument checkride immediately upon returning.
O In all, you complete **at least** 10 approaches, many with SID's, STAR's, & holding.
O You'll be astonished at how much you will learn in this total immersion experience.
O Aircraft owners: this is the ultimate insurance checkout if you need it.
O All of this adds up to a true flying adventure that will make you a more knowledgeable and confident pilot...plus it's a whole lot of fun!
O We know your aircraft—we've got time virtually all aircraft & helicopters and avionics configurations.

Prerequisites for Instrument Rating:

You'll be ready for an IPC or IFR check-ride immediately upon return if you have:
O a passing score on your instrument written,
O at least 50 hours PIC X/C & at least 40 hours of instrument time,
O and meet PTS requirements

Those that don't meet these requirements will receive instruction at reduced rate. This can be completed before or after the trip.

Availability:

This program starts every other Friday. Call for scheduling. Other routes and schedules are available for this highly individualized program.

Includes: All flight and ground instruction, over 35 hours combined. Orientation ground package including Checkride Review Guide

Not Included: Aircraft or anything related to the aircraft (Fuel, Oil, Insurance, Rental, Gov Fees, Repair, Etc), Meals, Ground Transportation & Lodging for you & your instructor, entertainment or any personal expenses you might encounter. You must supply your own aircraft, oil & fuel.

www.ifradventure.com

Introducing...

One of the most comprehensive Flight Training websites available

Resources for all pilots:

- Articles on current practices and techniques to help you fly safely (in the Reading section)
- Links to other websites.
- Download section.
- FAA Safety Publications, Manuals, Practical Test Standards, and Training Guides.
- Free question & answer on difficult aviation topics, answered by an expert.
- An online store to purchase training products for your rating.
- Information on aviation ground schools, including syllabus, schedule, and enrollment info.
- Information resources for getting back into flying, including information & structure of Flight Reviews (BFR) and Instrument Proficiency Checks (IPC).
- An extensive graphical & textual weather products page with thumbnail views of all the current weather.
- Human Factors for pro pilots

Resources for helicopter pilots:

- Complete syllabus online including a maneuvers checklist.
- Reading library, articles, and information on the various helicopter ratings.
- Helicopter Lesson Plans for helicopter students.

Resources for multi-engine pilots:

- Complete syllabus online including a maneuvers checklist.

www.cfidarren.com

Responsibility & Authority of the PIC (§91.3)

The PIC is directly responsible for and the final authority in determining the airworthiness and operation of the aircraft. The PIC may deviate from any FAR to meet the requirements of an emergency. If the PIC deviates from and FAR, he or she shall, if requested, send a written report of the deviation to the Administrator.

Flight Gear

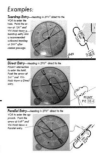

Visi-Hold™ - *Know Instantly*

Never wonder about holding entries again! Works with standard holds and non-standard holds (left turns). The Visi-Hold™ package comes complete with Visi-Hold™ template, directions, and two articles on holds: All About Holding and Holding Simplified. You'll pay no less than $14.95 for a complicated sliderule holding pattern calculator made by ASA. That's not even including shipping! Those of you who know what real IFR is like know that you can't fool around with a sliderule while the airplane is bouncing around. Instead, get the original Visi-Hold™, helping pilots know the holding pattern entry since 2000. Price: $10

Visi-Plotter™ - Simply the Best Flight Planning Plotter Made

This is the only VFR plotter invented by a CFI for pilots. It includes innovative features that provides temperature conversion, flight planning scratch pad area, and a no-mistakes course protractor that even beginners won't be confused by. It provides scales for sectional & WAC charts, and it even has inches & MM measurements. Price $15

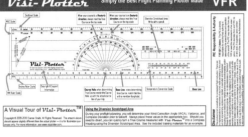

The Most Accurate

The Visi-Plotter navigational plotter is created from a calibrated hot stamp. It is the most accurate way to create a plotter. No other plotter on the market uses this production method because its more expensive than the silk screen method used by every other manufacturer.

Pilot's Rules of Thumb™ - the ultimate VFR/IFR Checklist

The ultimate checklist that every pilot needs. Ten years in development, this is a product that pilots of all levels of experience can immediately use. This tool covers 30 normal and non-normal situations and has 9 special tools that you'll use on every flight. This high-quality plastic ruler/checklist measures approximately 3.75" x 9". Click the picture to see a larger picture of this tool or click the link for more information. Price: $4

Online Ordering - Free Shipping
www.cfidarren.com

Publications

Using the NASA Form (PocketLearning)
Practical advice and tips using the NASA form when you've violated the FARs. This 48 page guide will walk you step by step through filing a NASA safety report. It will tell you the techniques and traps to submit a good report AND keep your pilot certificate unblemished. Price $12.

Winter Flying (PocketLearning)
Quick tips & techniques so you can get the most out of your winter flying - safely. Includes information on Winter Preflight, Induction Icing, Carb Icing, Airframe Icing, Tail Stalls, Hypothermia Strategies for Reducing the Risk, Winter Survival Kit, Aeronautical Decision Making, and the Personal Minimums Checklist. Size: 5" x 8" Price: $8

Aviation Acronyms (PocketLearning)
A complete pilot resource for aviation acronyms and contractions for every sector of aviation. Written by a pilot for pilots, this book provides instant answers to weather reports with confusing codes and aviation material with undefined acronyms. Designed to fit in your flight bag, size 5" x 8" Price: $12

Aviation Quotes (PocketLearning)
A collection of aviation's finest nuggets of knowledge distilled on the wings of time. Designed to fit in your flight bag, size 5" x 8" Price: $12

Guaranteed Pass Helicopter Flash Cards
This package includes 240 easy to read, soft yellow cards -- not flimsy paper -- which will help you pass your FAA written and oral (checkride) helicopter exams. Card size approximately: 4.25" x 2.75" - a stack of cards approximately 2" high. Includes all helicopter subjects. Price: $25

GUARANTEED PASS!
HELICOPTER
FLASH CARDS

Guaranteed Pass Glider Flash Cards
This is the product which will help you pass your FAA written and oral (checkride) glider exams. Includes all glider subjects. Card size approximately: 4.25" x 2.75" - Price: $25

Guaranteed Pass Balloon Flash Cards
This is the product which will help you pass your FAA written & oral (checkride) balloon exams. Includes all balloon subjects. Card size approximately: 4.25" x 2.75" - Price: $25

Practical Test Standards WITH Examiner's Notes
Don't just buy a regular PTS - buy the one with examiner's notes! Get the leg up on your checkride by knowing what will be asked during your oral exam. Also includes a chapter with additional reading material to help you put on your game face and sail through the checkride. Three versions to choose from.
- O   Private Pilot ASEL
- O   Commercial Pilot ASEL
- O   Instrument Rating

Online Ordering – Free Shipping
www.cfidarren.com

Instrument Rating Checkride Reviewer
Finally, instrument rating help! The best seller review guide is designed to help you to get through the Instrument Checkride. Includes a special offer for Visi-Hold™ (see other side) as a bonus. This package can be used as a self study guide or by flight instructors to provide IPC/Checkride preparation. Designed to fit in your flight bag, size: 6" x 9" Price: $25

Getting the Most from Your Flight Training
This is the essential guide to becoming a better pilot, paying the least, getting the most, and finishing as quickly as possible. Includes sections on Becoming a Better Pilot, Ground & Flight Instruction Tips, and Earning Certificates & Ratings. Designed to fit in your flight bag, size: 6" x 9" Price: $15

Pilot's Radio Communications Guide
This review guide is designed as a quick reference guide or radio communications training self study guide. This covers VFR & IFR radio communications. Build your confidence by knowing what to say and when. Designed to fit in your flight bag, size: 6" x 9" Price: $15

Learning IFR Enroute Charts
This 40 page guide helps the Flight Instructor or Instrument Students with IFR Enroute Symbology. It uses a unique IFR Chart Extract to teach symbology. It includes all symbology you need to know for your Instrument checkride or Instrument Proficiency Check. As a bonus chapter, Instrument Approach Procedure (plate) symbology is also included. All of which you need to know prior to your checkride. Price: $10

Safer Approaches
Safer Approaches will teach you how to conduct Instrument Approach Procedures to a higher standard of safety and precision. You will learn:
- Four Fundamentals of Safe Approaches,
- How to virtually eliminate possibility of Controlled Flight Into Terrain,
- How to perform a Constant Angle Non-Precision Approach (CANPA),
- How to calculate a Visual Descent Point (VDP),
- How to practice building your flying precision.
Includes the Stabilized Approach Descent Rate Table, a plastic, kneeboard sized IFR tool that will eliminate the mental math applying these techniques during your IFR flying.14pp. Price: $8

Practical Test Standards
A complete collection of FAA Practical Test Standards at budget prices.

Made in the USA
Thornton, CO
07/25/22 21:07:35

75b6fd35-50a7-42fc-a467-31fc0985d913R01